Flavour with HERBS

Herbs are among the oldest of ingredients used to add interest and flavour to food. The use of herbs in cooking, and in medicine and cosmetics, can be traced back to the earliest years of man's existence.

In this book you will find an exciting collection of recipes that show you just how easy herbs are to use, plus information on using, preserving and storing them for year-round flavour.

So whether it's a delicately flavoured tomato and thyme soup, a robust potato and pesto bake or the all-time favourite pizza you are sure to find a recipe to suit in this herb-flavoured selection.

CONTENTS

THE PANTRY SHELF

Unless otherwise stated, the following ingredients used in this book are:

Cream — Double, suitable for whipping

Flour — White flour, plain or standard

Sugar — White sugar

WHAT'S IN A TABLESPOON?

NEW ZEALAND
1 tablespoon =
15 mL OR 3 teaspoons

UNITED KINGDOM
1 tablespoon =
15 mL OR 3 teaspoons

AUSTRALIA
1 tablespoon =
20 mL OR 4 teaspoons

The recipes in this book were tested in Australia where a 20 mL tablespoon is standard. All measures are level.

The tablespoon in the New Zealand and United Kingdom sets of measuring spoons is 15 mL. In many recipes this difference will not matter. For recipes using baking powder, gelatine, bicarbonate of soda, small quantities of flour and cornflour, simply add another teaspoon for each tablespoon specified.

SOUPS

Nearly every soup is flavoured with herbs. This selection of soups highlights vegetable and herb combinations. To enhance the flavour, garnish soups with the herb used. Sprigs, flowers, whole or chopped leaves can all be used; they not only look wonderful but taste great.

Vegetable Soup with Pesto

VEGETABLE SOUP WITH PESTO

15 g/¹/₂ oz butter
1 small onion, chopped
1 leek, sliced
1 clove garlic, crushed
1 carrot, sliced
1 stalk celery, sliced
2 tomatoes, peeled and chopped
4 cabbage leaves, shredded
125 g/4 oz green beans, sliced
6 cups/1.5 litres/2¹/₂ pt chicken stock
60 g/2 oz grated Parmesan cheese

PESTO
125 g/4 oz fresh basil leaves
6 cloves garlic, crushed
1 tablespoon olive oil

1   To make Pesto, place basil leaves, garlic and oil in a food processor or blender and process until mixture is finely chopped. Spoon Pesto into an ice cube tray and freeze.

2   Melt butter in a large saucepan and cook onion, leek and garlic, stirring over a medium heat for 2-3 minutes or until onion is soft. Add carrot, celery, tomatoes, cabbage and beans and cook, stirring, for 3-4 minutes longer.

3   Stir in stock and bring to the boil. Reduce heat and simmer, uncovered, for 20 minutes or until vegetables are tender. To serve, ladle soup into heated bowls, place a Pesto cube in each bowl and sprinkle with Parmesan cheese.

Serves 6

Substantial enough to serve as a one-bowl meal, this soup is sure to be popular with family and friends. Just accompany with crusty wholegrain bread or rolls.

CHILLED CORIANDER YOGURT SOUP

500 g/1 lb natural yogurt
1 large bunch fresh coriander, leaves chopped
4 spring onions, finely chopped
1 cup/250 mL/8 fl oz cream (single)
3 cups/750 mL/1¹/₄ pt chicken stock

1   Place yogurt, coriander, spring onions and cream in a food processor or blender and process to combine.

2   Transfer yogurt mixture to a large bowl and stir in stock. Cover and chill for 2-3 hours or until ready to serve.

Serves 6

If you are using frozen chicken stock to make this soup, make sure that you bring the chicken stock to the boil, then chill it rapidly before making the soup. The quickest way to chill stock or soup is to transfer the hot liquid to a large cold bowl, then place the bowl in a sink of iced water. Stir stock or soup frequently and top up sink with additional ice cubes and water as required.

THYME AND LEEK SOUP

30 g/1 oz butter
2 large leeks, white part only, chopped
2 potatoes, chopped
2 teaspoons chopped fresh thyme
or $^1/_2$ teaspoon dried thyme
4 cups/1 litre/1$^3/_4$ pt chicken stock
4 tablespoons cream (double)
sprigs fresh thyme

Thyme is a highly fragrant herb of which there are many varieties. Common thyme is the one most used in cooking, but there are also lemon- , apple- and orange-scented thymes, to name but a few.

1   Melt butter in a large saucepan and cook leeks over a medium heat for 2-3 minutes. Add potatoes, thyme and stock. Bring to the boil, then reduce heat and simmer for 25 minutes or until potatoes are tender. Remove pan from heat and set aside to cool slightly.

2   Transfer soup mixture to a food processor or blender and process until smooth. Return soup to a clean saucepan and cook over a medium heat until hot. Ladle soup into warm bowls, place a tablespoon of cream in the centre of each bowl and swirl using a skewer. Garnish with thyme sprigs and serve immediately.

Serves 4

Thyme and Leek Soup

Dill and Carrot Soup

DILL AND CARROT SOUP

30 g/1 oz butter
1 large onion, chopped
1 large sweet potato or potato, chopped
3 large carrots, chopped
4 cups/1 litre/1^3/4 pt chicken
or vegetable stock
^{3}/4 cup/185 g/6 oz sour cream
2 tablespoons chopped fresh dill
sprigs fresh dill

Serves 4

1   Melt butter in a large saucepan and cook onion, sweet potato or potato and carrots for 5 minutes.

2   Stir in stock and bring to the boil, then reduce heat and simmer for 30 minutes. Remove pan from heat and set aside to cool slightly.

3   Transfer soup mixture, in batches, to a food processor or blender and process until smooth. To the last batch of soup mixture add the sour cream. Return soup to a clean saucepan and cook over a low heat, stirring constantly, until soup is hot. Do not allow the soup to boil or it will curdle. Stir in chopped dill and ladle soup into warmed bowls. Garnish with dill sprigs and serve immediately.

Dill and carrots have a natural affinity and no more so than in this delicious soup. This soup freezes well, but do not add the sour cream before freezing; stir it into the thawed soup just prior to reheating.

CREAMY TOMATO AND THYME SOUP

30 g/1 oz butter
2 onions, sliced
2 tablespoons finely chopped fresh
thyme or 2 teaspoons dried thyme
1 leek, sliced
2 stalks celery, sliced
2 x 440 g/14 oz canned tomatoes,
undrained and mashed
2 cups/500 mL/16 fl oz chicken stock
$^1/_4$ cup/60 mL/2 fl oz cream (double)
freshly ground black pepper
sprigs fresh thyme

1   Melt butter in a large saucepan and cook onions, thyme, leek and celery over a medium heat for 3-4 minutes or until vegetables are soft.

2   Stir in tomatoes and stock. Bring to the boil, then reduce heat and simmer for 30 minutes. Remove soup from heat and set aside to cool for 15 minutes. Place soup in a food processor or blender and process until smooth.

3   Return soup to a clean saucepan and heat over a medium heat for 4-5 minutes or until hot. Mix a little hot soup into cream, then mix cream mixture into soup. Season to taste with black pepper. Ladle soup into warm bowls, garnish with thyme sprigs and serve immediately.

Serves 4

Due to the acid content of tomatoes, creamy tomato soups have a tendency to curdle. To prevent this, mix a little of the hot soup with the cream before adding it to the soup.

CHILLED DILL SOUP

2 cups/500 mL/16 fl oz chicken
or vegetable stock
1 large onion, chopped
4 zucchini (courgettes), chopped
1 large potato, chopped
$^1/_2$ teaspoon ground cumin
1 cup/250 g/8 oz sour cream
2 tablespoons chopped fresh dill
sprigs fresh dill

1   Place stock, onion, zucchini (courgettes), potato and cumin in a large saucepan and bring to the boil. Reduce heat and simmer for 20 minutes or until potatoes are tender. Remove saucepan from heat and set aside to cool slightly.

2   Place soup mixture in a food processor or blender and process until smooth. Transfer soup to a large bowl, stir in sour cream and dill, then cover and chill for 3 hours before serving. Ladle soup into chilled bowls and garnish with dill sprigs.

Serves 4

This soup is also delicious served hot. To serve hot, place processed soup mixture, sour cream and dill in a saucepan and cook over a medium heat, stirring constantly, until soup is hot. Do not allow the soup to boil or it will curdle.

Creamy Tomato and Thyme Soup

CHILLED TOMATO SOUP

6 large ripe tomatoes, peeled
2 cups/500 mL/16 fl oz tomato juice
1 clove garlic, crushed
1 cucumber, peeled and chopped
4 spring onions, chopped
1 green pepper, chopped
2 stalks celery, chopped
1 tablespoon finely chopped fresh basil
freshly ground black pepper

1   Place tomatoes, tomato juice and garlic in a food processor or blender and process until smooth.

2   Transfer tomato mixture to a large bowl and stir in cucumber, spring onions, green pepper, celery, basil and black pepper to taste. Cover and refrigerate for 2-3 hours, or overnight, before serving.

Serves 6

This wonderful, uncooked soup is full of the tastes of summer. If possible, make it the day before to allow the flavours to develop. If good-flavoured fresh tomatoes are unavailable, you can make this soup using a can of undrained, peeled tomatoes.

STARTERS

Choose a starter from this array of herb-flavoured recipes for your next dinner party. Whether it's Gravadlax, the Scandinavian dish of salmon, or the Italian-inspired Tomato Pesto Slices, or Coriander Mussel Flans, you are sure to find something to suit any occasion.

Garlic and Rosemary
Prawns

Salmon and Chive
Pâté

Smoked Salmon Salad

Tomato Pesto Slices

Lime Sorbet

Carrot Timbales

Coriander Mussel Flans

Gravadlax

Garlic and Rosemary Prawns

GARLIC AND ROSEMARY PRAWNS

1 kg/2 lb large uncooked prawns,
shelled and deveined
2 cloves garlic, crushed
1 tablespoon olive oil
freshly ground black pepper
2 sprigs fresh rosemary
30 g/1 oz butter
1/2 cup/125 mL/4 fl oz dry vermouth

1 Place prawns, garlic, oil, black pepper to taste and rosemary in a large bowl and toss to combine. Cover and marinate in the refrigerator for 8 hours or overnight.

2 Melt butter in a large frying pan and cook prawns and marinade over a high heat for 2-3 minutes or until prawns change colour.

3 Using a slotted spoon, remove prawns from pan and set aside. Discard rosemary sprigs. Stir vermouth into pan, bring to the boil and boil until mixture reduces and forms a glaze. Return prawns to pan and toss to coat with glaze. Serve immediately.

Serves 4

While rosemary is most often associated with lamb, it is equally delicious with many other foods – including prawns – as you will discover when you cook this dish.

SALMON AND CHIVE PATE

2 teaspoons gelatine
2 tablespoons water
1/4 cup/60 mL/2 fl oz tarragon vinegar
3 egg yolks
125 g/4 oz butter
440 g/14 oz canned red salmon, drained,
bones and skin removed and flaked
4 tablespoons snipped fresh chives
freshly ground black pepper

1 Sprinkle gelatine over water in a small bowl, place it over a small saucepan of simmering water and stir until gelatine dissolves. Set aside to cool at room temperature.

2 Place vinegar in a small saucepan, bring to the boil and boil until reduced to 2 tablespoons. Set aside to cool. Place vinegar and egg yolks in a food processor or blender and process to combine. Melt butter until hot and bubbling, taking care not to let it burn. With food processor running, slowly pour in melted butter and process until thick.

3 Place salmon, gelatine and butter mixtures in a bowl and mix to combine. Stir in chives and season to taste with black pepper.

Serves 8

An easy pâté that is perfect for last-minute entertaining and is just as good made with pink salmon or tuna. The chives give it a wonderfully subtle onion flavour. The flowers of the chive plant are also edible and their mauve colour makes them a pretty garnish for soups, pâtés, dips and salads.

Smoked Salmon Salad

SMOKED SALMON SALAD

4 slices smoked salmon,
cut into strips
2 avocados, stoned, peeled
and thinly sliced
125 g/4 oz button mushrooms,
thinly sliced

DILL DRESSING
$^1/_4$ cup/60 mL/2 fl oz olive oil
$^1/_2$ teaspoon brown sugar
2 tablespoons freshly squeezed
lemon juice
1 tablespoon dry white wine
1 tablespoon chopped fresh dill

1   To make dressing, place oil, sugar,
lemon juice, wine and dill in a screwtop
jar and shake well to combine.

2   Place salmon, avocados and
mushrooms in a bowl, pour dressing over
and toss gently. Serve immediately.

Serves 4

Dill was taken to America by
the early settlers who called it
'meetin' seed' because the
dill seed was given to
children to chew on during
long Sunday sermons.

TOMATO PESTO SLICES

4 large tomatoes, cut into 12 thick slices
12 slices mozzarella cheese, cut
into rounds
6 slices cucumber, halved
6 black olives, pitted and halved
12 small sprigs fresh flat-leaved parsley

PESTO MAYONNAISE
1 large bunch fresh basil
1 clove garlic, crushed
60 g/2 oz pine nuts
2 tablespoons olive oil
2 tablespoons grated fresh
Parmesan cheese
2 tablespoons mayonnaise

1   To make mayonnaise, place basil leaves, garlic, pine nuts, oil and Parmesan cheese in a food processor or blender and process until smooth. Transfer mixture to a small bowl and stir in mayonnaise.

2   Top each tomato slice with a teaspoon of mayonnaise, then a slice of cheese, $^1/_2$ a slice of cucumber, $^1/_2$ an olive and a sprig of parsley.

Makes 12

Serve these strongly flavoured, pesto-topped tomato slices with crusty Italian bread, followed by pasta topped with a garlic tomato sauce and a tossed green salad.

Tomato Pesto Slices

LIME SORBET

1 cup/250 mL/8 fl oz fresh lime juice or
unsweetened lime cordial
1 cup/250 mL/8 fl oz water
12 fresh basil leaves, finely chopped
6 thin slices melon
sprigs watercress or small basil leaves

SUGAR SYRUP
1 cup/220 g/7 oz caster sugar
1 cup/250 mL/8 fl oz water

Crisp, citrus-flavoured sorbets
are excellent between-
course palate cleansers or
can be served as a refreshing
light dessert after a heavy or
spicy meal.

1   To make syrup, place sugar and water
in a saucepan and bring to the boil over a
medium heat. Reduce heat and simmer
for 10 minutes. Remove pan from heat
and set aside to cool before using.

2   Place syrup, lime juice or cordial,
water and basil leaves in a bowl and stir
to combine. Pour mixture into a shallow
freezerproof container, cover and place in
freezer until mixture is starting to freeze
around the edges.

3   Transfer sorbet mixture to a food
processor or blender and process until
smooth. Return mixture to a clean
freezerproof container, cover and freeze
until firm. Alternatively, this sorbet can
be made using an ice cream maker. Place
syrup, lime juice or cordial, water and
basil leaves in ice cream maker and freeze
following manufacturer's directions.

4   To serve, place scoops of sorbet in
glass bowls and garnish with melon slices
and watercress or basil leaves.

Serves 6

Lime Sorbet

Carrot Timbales

CARROT TIMBALES

6 carrots, sliced
30 g/1 oz butter
2 egg yolks
freshly ground black pepper
125 g/4 oz large spinach leaves

FRESH HERB SAUCE
15 g/$^1/_2$ oz butter
2 tablespoons flour
1 cup/250 mL/8 fl oz milk
1 tablespoon chopped fresh parsley
1 tablespoon snipped fresh chives
1 tablespoon chopped fresh mint
freshly ground black pepper

1 Boil, steam or microwave carrots until tender. Drain and set aside to cool. Place carrots, butter and egg yolks in a food processor or blender and process until smooth. Season to taste with black pepper.

2 Lightly blanch spinach leaves and use to line six lightly greased timbale moulds or ramekins, allowing some of the leaves to overhang the top. Spoon carrot mixture into moulds and fold spinach leaves over to cover mixture. Cook for 25-30 minutes or until set.

3 To make sauce, melt butter in a saucepan, stir in flour and cook, stirring, for 1 minute. Gradually whisk in milk and cook over a medium heat, stirring constantly, until sauce boils and thickens. Add parsley, chives and mint, and season to taste with black pepper. Serve hot sauce with timbales.

Serves 6

Oven temperature
200°C, 400°F, Gas 6

The herb sauce that accompanies these colourful timbales is also delicious served with boiled, steamed or microwaved vegetables and fish.

CORIANDER MUSSEL FLANS

Oven temperature
220°C, 425°F, Gas 7

The ancient Chinese believed that anyone who ate coriander would enjoy immortality; in the Middle East and Europe, coriander has long been valued as a love potion and aphrodisiac.

PASTRY
1^1/2 cups/185 g/6 oz flour
^{1}/4 teaspoon baking powder
125 g/4 oz butter, cubed and chilled
1 egg yolk
1-2 tablespoons iced water
^{1}/2 teaspoon lemon juice

MUSSEL FILLING
16 mussels, in shells, scrubbed
and debearded
1 leek, cut into thin strips
2 large carrots, cut into thin strips
1 tablespoon finely chopped
fresh coriander
1^1/4 cups/315 mL/10 fl oz
cream (double)
12 uncooked prawns, peeled
and deveined
6 teaspoons flour
30 g/1 oz butter
freshly ground black pepper

1 To make pastry, place flour, baking powder and butter in a food processor or blender and process until mixture resembles coarse bread crumbs. Combine egg yolk, water and lemon juice. With machine running, gradually pour in egg mixture, until a soft dough forms. Turn dough onto a lightly floured surface and knead gently. Wrap dough in plastic food wrap and refrigerate for 1 hour.

2 Divide pastry into four portions and roll out thinly on a lightly floured surface. Line four 10 cm/4 in flan tins with pastry and prick base of each flan with a fork. Line flans with nonstick baking paper and fill with uncooked rice. Bake for 5 minutes, remove paper and rice, and bake for 12 minutes longer.

3 To make filling, place mussels in a large saucepan, add just enough water to cover and cook over a low heat until shells open. Discard any mussels that have not opened. Using a slotted spoon remove mussels from liquid. Remove mussel meat from shells and discard shells. Reserve ^{1}/2 cup/125 mL/4 fl oz of pan liquid. Heat reserved liquid in a frying pan, add leek, carrots and coriander, and cook for 2 minutes.

4 Stir in cream, prawns and mussels, and cook over a low heat for 5 minutes. Mix flour and butter together to form a paste, then whisk small quantities of paste into cream mixture and cook, stirring, for 2-3 minutes or until thickened and smooth. Season to taste with black pepper. Spoon filling into warm pastry cases and serve immediately.

Serves 4

Coriander Mussel Flans

14

Gravadlax

GRAVADLAX

750 g/1¹/₂ lb salmon fillet, bones
and skin removed
2 cups/500 mL/16 fl oz rosé wine
2 teaspoons finely grated orange rind
2 teaspoons finely grated lime rind
2 tablespoons chopped fresh coriander
1 tablespoon cracked black pepper
2 tablespoons chopped fresh dill
4 tablespoons coarse sea salt
¹/₂ cup/90 g/3 oz brown sugar
¹/₂ cup/125 mL/4 fl oz olive oil

Serves 6

1 Place salmon in a shallow dish.
Place wine, orange rind and lime rind
in a small bowl, mix to combine and
pour over salmon. Cover and refrigerate
for 24 hours.

2 Remove salmon from wine mixture
and pat dry using absorbent kitchen
paper. Place coriander, black pepper, dill,
salt and sugar in a small bowl and mix to
combine. Brush salmon with half the oil
and sprinkle with half the coriander
mixture. Place salmon herbed side down
on a large piece of aluminium foil. Brush
other side with remaining oil and sprinkle
with remaining coriander mixture. Wrap
salmon tightly in foil and refrigerate for 2
days. Serve cut into thin slices.

While this dish needs to
be prepared several days
ahead, you will be well
pleased with the result.
Gravadlax makes a
delicious first course served
with thin slices of lemon and
rye bread.

MAIN MEALS

Many of our favourite dishes rely on herbs for their distinctive flavours. This selection of main meal ideas will show you how to make the most of herbs and give you new ideas and inspiration. Why not try the Rosemary Chicken Pie or the Coriander Beef Salad for dinner tonight?

HERB SCHNITZELS

4 lean veal or pork
schnitzels (escalopes)
$^{1}/_{4}$ cup/60 mL/2 fl oz lemon juice
$^{1}/_{4}$ cup/60 mL/2 fl oz dry vermouth
3 tablespoons vegetable oil
$^{3}/_{4}$ cup/90 g/3 oz dried bread crumbs
1 tablespoon chopped fresh rosemary or
1 teaspoon dried rosemary
1 tablespoon chopped fresh parsley
flour
1 egg, lightly beaten
30 g/1 oz butter
2 teaspoons cornflour blended with
$^{1}/_{2}$ cup/125 mL/4 fl oz cream (double)
or evaporated milk

1   Trim veal of all visible fat and place in a shallow dish. Combine lemon juice, vermouth and 2 tablespoons oil. Pour over veal and set aside to marinate for 10-15 minutes.

2   Drain meat and reserve marinade. Combine bread crumbs, rosemary and parsley and place in a shallow dish. Place flour in a plastic food bag, add veal and shake to coat. Shake excess flour from veal, then dip in egg and coat with bread crumb mixture.

3   Heat butter and 1 tablespoon oil in a frying pan and cook veal for 2-3 minutes each side or until golden. Remove from pan, set aside and keep warm.

4   Drain pan of excess fat and pour in reserved marinade. Bring to the boil and boil until liquid has reduced by half, whisk in cornflour mixture and cook, stirring, until sauce thickens. Spoon sauce over veal and serve immediately.

Serves 4

For something different you might like to replace the rosemary in this recipe with thyme, oregano or marjoram. Serve these tasty schnitzels (escalopes) with a stir-fry of leeks, mushrooms and pumpkin or carrot, or a tossed green salad and baked potatoes.

BARBECUED LAMB

1 x 1.5-2 kg/3-4 lb boned leg of lamb
2 cloves garlic, cut into slivers
2 sprigs fresh rosemary
freshly ground black pepper

LEMON HERB BUTTER
125 g/4 oz butter, softened
2 teaspoons finely grated lemon rind
1 tablespoon chopped fresh basil
1 tablespoon chopped fresh parsley
1 tablespoon lemon juice
1 teaspoon sweet chilli sauce

1   Preheat barbecue to a medium heat. Trim meat of all excess fat. Using a sharp knife, make three deep slashes in top of meat and tuck slivers of garlic and rosemary leaves into each. Sprinkle liberally with black pepper.

2   To make Lemon Herb Butter, place butter, lemon rind, basil, parsley, lemon juice and chilli sauce in a small bowl and mix well to combine.

3   Spread some of the Lemon Herb Butter over the lamb. Cook lamb on lightly oiled barbecue grill, turning several times and basting with Lemon Herb Butter for 45-60 minutes or until cooked to your liking.

Just the thing for outdoor entertaining, this barbecued leg of lamb is easy to prepare and more or less looks after itself once it is on the barbecue. All you need to do is baste it a few times and turn it over. Serve with baked potatoes – these can cook on the barbecue with the lamb. Choose medium-sized potatoes, wrap in aluminium foil and allow about 60 minutes cooking time. Barbecued tomatoes and a salad of mixed lettuces and fresh herbs would complete this summer meal.

Herb Schnitzels

Serves 8

BARBECUED SALMON WITH DILL BASTE

90 g/3 oz butter
1 clove garlic, crushed
$^1/_4$ cup/60 mL/2 fl oz lime or lemon juice
2 teaspoons finely grated lime
or lemon rind
1 tablespoon dry white wine
2 teaspoons honey
freshly ground black pepper
1 tablespoon chopped fresh dill
4 x 185 g/6 oz pieces salmon fillet

1   Melt butter, over a medium heat, in a small saucepan and cook garlic for 1 minute. Stir in lime or lemon juice, rind, wine, honey and black pepper to taste. Remove pan from heat and add dill.

2   Preheat barbecue to a medium heat. Brush salmon with dill mixture and cook, basting with dill mixture, on lightly oiled barbecue grill for 3-4 minutes each side or until fish flakes when tested with a fork.

Serves 4

This recipe can also be cooked under the grill. The cooking time is 2-3 minutes each side, depending on the heat of the grill and the thickness of the fillets.

Barbecued Salmon with Dill Baste

HERB-CRUSTED RACK OF LAMB

Herb-crusted Rack of Lamb

2 racks of lamb, each containing 6 cutlets

HERB CRUST
1 cup/60 g/2 oz bread crumbs, made from stale bread
4 tablespoons chopped fresh parsley
2 tablespoons chopped fresh rosemary or 2 teaspoons dried rosemary
1 clove garlic, crushed
2 tablespoons Dijon-style mustard
2 tablespoons olive oil
freshly ground black pepper

1 To make crust, place bread crumbs, parsley, rosemary, garlic, mustard, oil and black pepper to taste in a bowl and mix to combine. Set aside.

2 Place lamb racks in a lightly greased baking dish and bake for 15 minutes. Remove dish from oven and press crust mixture onto top of lamb racks.

3 Return lamb to the oven and bake for 10-15 minutes longer or until lamb is cooked to your liking and crust is golden.

Serves 4

Oven temperature
180°C, 350°F, Gas 4

Rack of lamb is a popular choice for busy people – it cooks quickly, is easy to prepare and tastes delicious.

19

Potato Kransky Salad

500 g/1 lb baby potatoes, peeled
and halved
3 tablespoons vegetable oil
4 Kransky or Polish sausages
250 g/8 oz asparagus spears, cut
into
3 cm/1¹/4 in pieces
3 spring onions, chopped
CHIVE DRESSING
2 tablespoons snipped fresh chives
1 clove garlic, crushed
2 teaspoons lemon juice
¹/4 cup/45 g/1¹/2 oz natural yogurt
¹/4 cup/60 g/2 oz sour cream
freshly ground black pepper

1   Boil or microwave potatoes until just tender. Drain, then toss in 2 tablespoons oil. Place in a baking dish and bake, turning occasionally, for 20 minutes or until golden.

2   Heat remaining oil in a frying pan and cook sausages until golden and cooked through. Remove from pan, drain on absorbent kitchen paper, allow to cool then cut into slices.

3   Add asparagus and spring onions to frying pan and stir-fry for 2-3 minutes or until asparagus changes colour and is just tender. Drain and set aside to cool. Place potatoes, sausages and asparagus mixture in a bowl and toss gently to combine.

4   To make dressing, place chives, garlic, lemon juice, yogurt, sour cream and black pepper to taste in a food processor or blender and process until smooth.

Serves 4

To serve, divide salad between four plates and spoon over dressing. While this is a complete meal, you might also like to serve crusty bread or rolls for very hungry people.
Kransky or Polish sausages are available from continental delicatessens and some butchers.

Coriander Beef Salad

500 g/1 lb rump steak
1 bunch watercress or 1 lettuce
¹/2 red pepper, cut into thin strips

CORIANDER DRESSING
2 cloves garlic, crushed
4 tablespoons chopped fresh coriander
3 tablespoons chopped fresh mint leaves
2 tablespoons olive oil
1 teaspoon chilli paste (sambal oelek)
2 tablespoons lime juice
2 teaspoons fish sauce
2 teaspoons brown sugar
¹/2 teaspoon ground cumin
freshly ground black pepper

1   Cook steak under a preheated grill for 3-4 minutes each side or until medium rare. Remove steak from grill and set aside to cool. Cut cold steak into slices across the grain.

2   To make dressing, place garlic, coriander, mint, oil, chilli paste (sambal oelek), lime juice, fish sauce, sugar, cumin and black pepper to taste in a food processor or blender and process to combine.

3   Arrange watercress, or lettuce, and steak on a serving platter, drizzle dressing over and garnish with red pepper strips.

Serves 4

Coriander is a herb you either love or hate. If you fall into the second category you could make this salad using parsley in place of the coriander.

Potato Kransky Salad
Coriander Beef Salad

FRUITY PORK SALAD

15 g/¹/₂ oz butter
1 tablespoon vegetable oil
1.5 kg/3 lb pork fillets
60 g/2 oz dried apricots, chopped
185 g/6 oz pitted prunes
90 g/3 oz sultanas
3 spring onions, cut diagonally
into 2 cm/³/₄ in pieces
3 large green apples, cored and cut into
2 cm/³/₄ in cubes

PARSLEY DRESSING
¹/₂ cup/125 mL/4 fl oz olive oil
2 tablespoons lemon juice
2 tablespoons vinegar
1 tablespoon French mustard
2 teaspoons brown sugar
2 tablespoons chopped fresh parsley
freshly ground black pepper

1   Heat butter and vegetable oil in a frying pan and cook pork fillets over a high heat until brown on all sides. Transfer pork to a baking dish and bake for 15 minutes or until cooked. Remove from dish and set aside to cool. Reserve pan juices.

2   Place apricots and prunes in separate bowls and pour over boiling water to cover. Set aside to soak for 30 minutes.

3   Heat reserved pan juices in frying pan and cook sultanas, spring onions and apples over a medium heat for 5 minutes or until apples are soft. Transfer to a large bowl. Drain apricots and prunes and add to apple mixture. Cut pork into slices and add to fruit mixture.

4   To make dressing, place olive oil, lemon juice, vinegar, mustard, sugar, parsley and black pepper to taste in a screwtop jar and shake well to combine. Pour over salad and toss to combine.

Serves 8

While parsley is probably the best known and most used herb, its exact origin is unknown. It is thought to have come from Sardinia and was used by the ancient Greeks and Romans. The Romans made garlands of parsley for banquet guests and ate large quantities in an attempt to prevent drunkenness!

Fruity Pork Salad

BASIL AND PORK PIZZA

Basil and Pork Pizza

315 g/10 oz lean pork mince
2 tablespoons chopped fresh basil
2 cloves garlic, crushed
4 spring onions, chopped
freshly ground black pepper
3 tablespoons tomato paste (purée)
125 g/4 oz grated mozzarella cheese
1 red pepper, cut into rings
12 black olives, pitted
2 tablespoons chopped fresh parsley

PIZZA BASE
$^3/_4$ cup/185 g/6 oz corn meal (polenta)
$^1/_2$ cup/60 g/2 oz self-raising flour
1 teaspoon baking powder
155 mL/5 fl oz milk

1   To make base, place corn meal (polenta), flour and baking powder in a large bowl. Make a well in the centre and gradually pour in milk, mixing to form a sticky dough. Turn dough onto a lightly floured surface and knead for 3-4 minutes. Press into a greased 23 cm/9 in pizza tray, bringing up the edges to form a rim.

2   Place pork, basil, garlic, spring onions and black pepper to taste in a bowl and mix to combine. Set aside. Spread pizza base with tomato paste (purée) and top with meat mixture and half the cheese. Arrange red pepper rings and olives attractively on pizza, then sprinkle with remaining cheese and parsley. Bake for 45 minutes or until pizza is cooked.

Serves 6

Oven temperature
180°C, 350°F, Gas 4

A member of the mint family, basil is one of the world's oldest herbs. It is believed to be native to Thailand and India. Indian Hindus consider sacred basil to be the most sacred plant of all and believe it to be a protection against evil – Hindus are buried with a basil leaf.

BEEF WITH LEMON GRASS

2 tablespoons vegetable oil
2 onions, chopped
1 teaspoon whole allspice
1 x 5 cm/2 in cinnamon stick
1 teaspoon grated fresh ginger
2 green peppers, cut into strips
750 g/1^1/$_2$ lb chuck steak, cut into
2.5 cm/1 in cubes
2 tablespoons chopped fresh lemon grass
or 3 teaspoons dried lemon grass
2 cups/500 mL/16 fl oz chicken stock
500 g/1 lb pumpkin or carrot, peeled
and cut into 2.5 cm/1 in cubes
2 cloves garlic, crushed
freshly ground black pepper

1   Heat oil in a large heavy-based saucepan and cook onions over a medium heat for 10 minutes or until golden. Stir in allspice, cinnamon stick, ginger and green pepper and cook for 1 minute longer.

2   Add meat to pan and cook over a high heat for 4-5 minutes or until browned on all sides. Stir in lemon grass and stock, bring to the boil, then reduce heat, cover and simmer for 45 minutes.

3   Add pumpkin or carrot to pan. Cover and simmer for 45 minutes longer or until beef and pumpkin are tender. Remove pan from heat, stir in garlic and season to taste with black pepper.

Serves 6

Lemon grass is a tender, lemon-scented grass of the tropics. Much used in Southeast Asian cooking, it is available fresh or dried from oriental specialty shops. If you cannot obtain it, use finely grated lemon peel instead.

SAUSAGE RAGOUT

12 baby potatoes, scrubbed
12 baby onions
^{1}/$_4$ cup/60 mL/2 fl oz soy sauce
^{1}/$_2$ cup/125 mL/4 fl oz lemon juice
1 cup/250 mL/8 fl oz beef stock
1 cup/250 mL/8 fl oz dry white wine
3 tablespoons chopped fresh basil

HERBED SAUSAGES
500 g/1 lb lean beef mince
4 tablespoons chopped fresh parsley
4 tablespoons chopped fresh basil
3 tablespoons pine nuts
1 tablespoon olive oil
2 cloves garlic, crushed
3 cups/185 g/6 oz bread crumbs, made
from stale bread
3 tablespoons grated Parmesan cheese
freshly ground black pepper
seasoned flour
oil for deep-frying

1   To make sausages, place mince, parsley, basil, pine nuts, oil, garlic, bread crumbs, Parmesan cheese and black pepper to taste in a large bowl and mix to combine. Shape mixture into twelve sausages, each 10 cm/4 in long. Roll each sausage in seasoned flour and set aside.

2   Heat oil in a large saucepan and cook sausages a few at a time until browned, but not cooked through. Remove sausages and drain on absorbent kitchen paper.

3   Place sausages, potatoes and onions in a large saucepan. Place soy sauce, lemon juice, stock, wine and basil in a bowl and mix to combine. Pour over sausages in saucepan, bring to the boil, then reduce heat, cover and simmer for 20 minutes or until potatoes and onions are tender.

Serves 6

For a complete meal, serve this tasty ragout with a chilled tomato salad and crusty French bread.

GARLIC FISH SALAD

30 g/1 oz butter
1 clove garlic, crushed
500 g/1 lb firm white fish fillets, cut
into 2.5 cm/1 in cubes
1 bunch watercress

GREEN AIOLI
3 egg yolks
4 tablespoons chopped fresh parsley
4 tablespoons chopped fresh basil
2 tablespoons snipped fresh chives
2 tablespoons lemon juice
1 clove garlic, crushed
1 cup/250 mL/8 fl oz olive oil

1   To make aioli, place egg yolks, parsley, basil, chives, lemon juice and garlic in a food processor or blender and, with machine running, slowly add oil in a steady stream until a mayonnaise of a thick consistency forms.

2   Melt butter in a large frying pan and cook garlic over a medium heat for 1 minute. Add fish and cook for 3-4 minutes or until fish flakes when tested with a fork.

3   Serve fish on a bed of watercress topped with aioli.

Serves 4

Garlic is different to many herbs in that it is the bulb of the plant that is used, not the leaves.
Many superstitions, myths and stories surround garlic. In Eastern Europe, hanging garlic on the door of your house or around your neck was considered to be the best way to deter vampires.

Beef with Lemon Grass,
Sausage Ragout

Mushroom Baskets

Oven temperature
200°C, 400°F, Gas 6

These delicious bread
baskets make wonderful
containers for all sorts of
different foods. You might
like to try filling them with
creamy curried vegetables
or with salad.

Mushroom Baskets

1 loaf unsliced wholemeal bread
vegetable oil

MUSHROOM FILLING
30 g/1 oz butter
1 clove garlic, crushed
1 teaspoon ground cumin
2 small zucchini (courgettes), cut
into 5 cm/2 in sticks
185 g/6 oz button mushrooms
125 g/4 oz flat mushrooms
125 g/4 oz oyster mushrooms
juice 1 lemon
6 spring onions, cut into
5 cm/2 in pieces
2 tablespoons finely chopped fresh mint
freshly ground black pepper

Serves 6

1   Remove crusts from bread and cut
into six thick slices. Remove centre from
each slice, leaving bases intact to form
baskets. Brush all surfaces with oil and
bake for 10-15 minutes or until baskets
are golden.

2   To make filling, melt butter in a large
frying pan and cook garlic and cumin
over a medium heat for 1-2 minutes. Add
zucchini (courgettes) and stir-fry for 3-4
minutes. Remove vegetable mixture from
pan and set aside.

3   Place button, flat and oyster
mushrooms and lemon juice in a bowl
and toss to combine. Add mushroom
mixture to pan and cook for 3-4 minutes.
Return zucchini mixture and spring
onions to pan and cook for 2-3 minutes
longer. Stir in chopped mint and season
to taste with black pepper. Spoon
mushroom filling into bread baskets and
garnish with mint sprigs.

ROSEMARY CHICKEN PIE

CHEESE PASTRY
2 cups/250 g/8 oz flour, sifted
60 g/2 oz grated tasty cheese
(mature Cheddar)
1 teaspoon dry mustard
$^1/_2$ teaspoon cayenne pepper
185 g/6 oz butter, chilled and cut
into small cubes
1 egg yolk, lightly beaten
3-4 tablespoons chilled water

ROSEMARY CHICKEN FILLING
1 tablespoon olive oil
750 g/1$^1/_2$ lb boneless chicken
breast fillets, chopped
60 g/2 oz butter
1 clove garlic, crushed
1 stalk celery, chopped
1 onion, chopped
$^1/_4$ cup/30 g/1 oz flour
1 cup/250 mL/8 fl oz chicken stock
1 cup/250 mL/8 fl oz milk
1 tablespoon chopped fresh parsley
1 tablespoon chopped fresh rosemary or
1 teaspoon dried rosemary
freshly ground black pepper

1   To make pastry, place flour, cheese, mustard, cayenne pepper and butter in a food processor and process until mixture resembles coarse bread crumbs. With machine running, add egg yolk and enough water to form a soft dough. Turn dough onto a lightly floured surface and knead gently until smooth. Wrap in plastic food wrap and refrigerate for 30 minutes.

2   To make filling, heat oil in a large frying pan and cook chicken in batches over a high heat until cooked through. Remove chicken from pan and set aside.

3   Melt butter in frying pan and cook garlic, celery and onion, over a medium heat, for 3-4 minutes, or until onion is soft. Stir in flour and cook for 1 minute longer. Remove pan from heat and stir in stock and milk. Return pan to heat, bring to the boil, stirring constantly, and simmer for 3 minutes. Add chicken, parsley and rosemary to sauce and season to taste with black pepper. Set aside to cool completely.

4   Place cold filling in a 23 cm/9 in pie dish. On a lightly floured surface roll out pastry to 5 mm/$^1/_4$ in thickness. Brush rim of pie dish with a little water and place the pastry over the filling. Trim edges with a knife and decorate top of pie as desired. Brush top of pie with a little milk and bake for 30-35 minutes or until pastry is cooked and golden and filling is hot.

Serves 6

Oven temperature
200°C, 400°F, Gas 6

The herb of remembrance, rosemary was worn on the heads of Greek scholars to help them retain information. According to legend, 'Rosemary will not grow well unless the mistress of the house is the master'.

Rosemary Chicken Pie

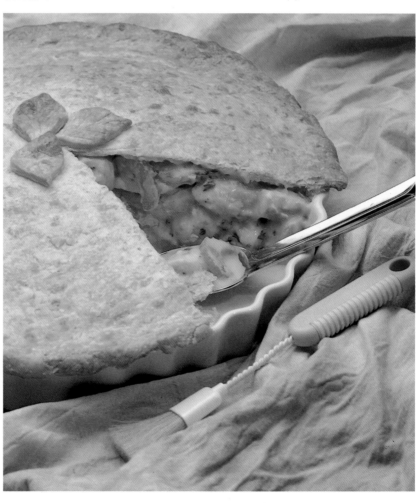

CORIANDER-FILLED PORK

Oven temperature
250°C, 500°F, Gas 9

1 x 1.5 kg/3 lb boned pork loin

CORIANDER STUFFING
2^1/$_2$ cups/155 g/5 oz bread crumbs,
made from stale bread
2 cloves garlic, crushed
1 tablespoon finely grated lemon rind
4 tablespoons chopped fresh coriander
1 egg, beaten
60 g/2 oz butter, melted
freshly ground black pepper

1   To make stuffing, place bread crumbs, garlic, lemon rind and coriander in a bowl and mix to combine. Mix in egg and butter and season to taste with black pepper.

2   Unroll loin and make a cut in the middle of the fleshy part of the meat, to make a space for the stuffing. Score the rind with a sharp knife.

3   Spread stuffing over cut flap. Roll up loin firmly and secure with string. Place in a baking dish. Rub rind with salt and bake for 20 minutes. Reduce oven temperature to 180°C/350°F/Gas 4 and bake for 1 hour longer or until juices run clear when tested with a skewer in the meatiest part.

Serves 8

A roast with a difference. Accompany with roasted carrots and parsnips, baby new potatoes and green beans or asparagus.

TUNA WITH CHILLI HERB SAUCE

60 g/2 oz butter
4 tuna steaks
^{1}/$_4$ cup/60 mL/2 fl oz white wine
^{1}/$_4$ cup/60 mL/2 fl oz cream (double)
1 tablespoon chopped mixed fresh herbs,
such as parsley, chives,
coriander and basil
1 teaspoon chilli paste (sambal oelek)

1   Melt butter in a large frying pan and cook tuna steaks over a medium heat for 3 minutes each side or until flesh flakes when tested with a fork. Transfer steaks to a warm plate, set aside and keep warm.

2   Add wine to pan, increase heat to high and cook for 1 minute. Stir in cream, reduce heat and simmer for 1-2 minutes or until sauce thickens slightly. Stir in herbs and chilli paste (sambal oelek). Spoon sauce over tuna steaks and serve immediately.

Serves 4

These tuna steaks are delicious served with a tossed green salad and crusty wholemeal rolls.
If tuna steaks are unavailable you might like to use cod, halibut or groper steaks.

Coriander-filled Pork

SAGE BEEF SALAD

2 tablespoons vegetable oil
750 g/1^1/$_2$ lb piece sirloin or rump steak
2 onions, sliced
2 cloves garlic, crushed
2 carrots, chopped
1 bay leaf
1 stalk celery, chopped
4 cups/1 litre/1^3/$_4$ pt boiling beef stock
6 small dill pickles, sliced
thinly lengthwise
1 tablespoon capers
1 cucumber, sliced
^{1}/$_4$ red pepper, cut into thin strips

SAGE DRESSING
^{1}/$_2$ cup/125 mL/4 fl oz olive oil
^{1}/$_4$ cup/60 mL/2 fl oz lemon juice
1 tablespoon chopped fresh thyme or
1 teaspoon dried thyme
2 cloves garlic, crushed
1 tablespoon chopped fresh sage
1 tablespoon Dijon-style mustard
freshly ground black pepper

1   Heat oil in a large saucepan and cook meat over a high heat until brown on all sides. Remove meat from pan and set aside. Add onions, garlic, carrots, bay leaf and celery to pan and cook, stirring, over a medium heat for 10 minutes. Return meat to pan and place on top of vegetables. Pour in boiling stock, cover and simmer for 2-2^1/$_2$ hours or until meat is tender. Remove pan from heat and allow beef to cool in liquid, then refrigerate until ready to serve.

2   To make dressing, place oil, lemon juice, thyme, garlic, sage, mustard and black pepper to taste in a screwtop jar and shake well to combine.

3   To assemble salad, slice beef thinly. Place beef, dill pickles, capers and cucumber in a bowl. Pour dressing over and toss gently to combine. Transfer to a large serving platter and garnish with red pepper strips.

Sage has long been valued for its powers of longevity; an ancient proverb in many parts of the world goes along the lines, 'How can a man grow old who has sage in his garden?'.

Sage Beef Salad

Serves 6

GRILLED FISH WITH MANDARIN SALSA

Grilled Fish with Mandarin Salsa

6 x 155 g/5 oz fish cutlets
310 g/10 oz canned mandarin segments,
drained and juice reserved
30 g/1 oz butter

CORIANDER MARINADE
reserved mandarin juice
3 tablespoons chopped fresh coriander
3 tablespoons chopped fresh parsley
1 teaspoon chilli paste (sambal oelek)
$^1/_2$ teaspoon ground cumin
$^1/_4$ cup/60 mL/2 fl oz lime or
lemon juice
2 tablespoons white wine

Serves 6

1 To make marinade, place mandarin juice, coriander, parsley, chilli paste (sambal oelek), cumin, lime or lemon juice and wine in a bowl and mix to combine.

2 Place fish cutlets in a single layer in a shallow dish and pour marinade over. Cover and set aside to marinate for 1-2 hours. Drain fish and reserve marinade.

3 Cook fish cutlets under a preheated grill or on a preheated barbecue for 3-4 minutes each side or until flesh flakes when tested with a fork.

4 Place reserved marinade and mandarin segments in a small saucepan and bring to simmering. Remove saucepan from heat and stir in butter. Serve with fish.

The combination of coriander and chilli in this fish dish is reminiscent of Asian cuisine. Serve with boiled or steamed white or brown rice and a stir-fry of mixed vegetables.

31

BEEF TOMATO AND BASIL CASSEROLE

2 tablespoons olive oil
1 kg/2 lb chuck steak, trimmed of all
visible fat and cut into 2 cm/³/4 in cubes
2 onions, roughly chopped
4 cloves garlic, crushed
250 g/8 oz button mushrooms
3 tablespoons pine nuts
1 cup/250 mL/8 fl oz white wine
1 tablespoon chopped fresh basil or
1 teaspoon dried basil
2 x 440 g/14 oz canned tomatoes,
undrained and mashed
3 tablespoons tomato paste (purée)
¹/2 teaspoon brown sugar
2 tablespoons Worcestershire sauce
1 tablespoon sweet fruit chutney
freshly ground black pepper

Just prior to serving, you may like to sprinkle the casserole with additional toasted pine nuts. Serve with boiled noodles tossed with chopped parsley and freshly ground black pepper and a green vegetable such as beans or zucchini (courgettes).

1   Heat oil in a large frying pan and cook beef over a high heat until browned. Reduce heat and add onions, garlic, mushrooms and pine nuts. Cook, stirring constantly, until onions are soft and pine nuts golden.

2   Stir in wine and basil, bring to simmering and simmer for 5 minutes, scraping up bits from base of pan. Add tomatoes, tomato paste (purée), sugar, Worcestershire sauce and chutney. Cover, bring to simmering and simmer for 1¹/2-2 hours or until meat is tender. Season to taste with black pepper.

Serves 6

MINTED TANDOORI CUTLETS

8 lamb chump chops, each
cut into 3 pieces
1 tablespoon chopped fresh mint

TANDOORI MARINADE
1 cup/200 g/6¹/2 oz natural yogurt
1 tablespoon ground cumin
1 tablespoon ground coriander
2 tablespoons curry powder
freshly ground black pepper

1   To make marinade, place yogurt, cumin, coriander, curry powder and black pepper to taste in a bowl and mix to combine. Add lamb pieces and toss to coat. Cover and set aside to marinate for 1-2 hours or overnight in the refrigerator.

2   Place lamb pieces on a rack set in a baking dish and bake, turning every 15 minutes, for 45 minutes or until lamb is tender. Sprinkle lamb with mint and serve immediately.

Serves 4

Oven temperature
180°C, 350°F, Gas 4

Serve with boiled white or brown rice and a salad of tomatoes and mint. To make the tomato salad, thinly slice 4 tomatoes and 1 onion. Arrange on a platter and sprinkle with a little herb vinegar, a little vegetable oil and 1 tablespoon finely chopped fresh mint.

Minted Tandoori Cutlets

LIGHT MEALS

*Pasta, eggs and cheese form the basis of many
light meals. When they are flavoured with herbs you will find
the ordinary becomes the extraordinary. Next time you need a
quick dinner or light lunch why not try a Cheesy Herb
Soufflé or Tabbouleh Tomatoes?*

Herb and Vegetable
Fettuccine

Parsley Brains

Gnocchi with Herb
Sauce

Cheesy Herb Soufflé

Quick Calamari
and Mint

Dill and Seafood
Ragout

Chive and Cheese
Croquettes

Tabbouleh Tomatoes

Coriander Beef Pittas

Leek and Dill Tart

Herb and Vegetable Fettuccine

HERB AND VEGETABLE FETTUCCINE

30 g/1 oz dried mushrooms
boiling water
250 g/8 oz fettuccine
2 tablespoons olive oil
2 cloves garlic, crushed
250 g/8 oz asparagus, cut into
2.5 cm/1 in lengths
$^1/_2$ red pepper, chopped
125 g/4 oz prosciutto or bacon,
cut into strips
30 g/1 oz small basil leaves
1 tablespoon lemon juice
freshly ground black pepper
4 tablespoons grated Parmesan cheese

1   Place mushrooms in a bowl and cover with boiling water. Set aside to soak for 20 minutes or until mushrooms are tender. Drain, remove stalks if necessary and chop mushrooms.

2   Cook fettuccine in boiling water in a large saucepan following packet directions. Drain, set aside and keep warm.

3   Heat oil in a large frying pan and cook mushrooms and garlic over a medium heat for 2 minutes. Add asparagus, red pepper and prosciutto or bacon and cook for 2-3 minutes longer.

4   Stir in basil leaves, lemon juice and fettuccine and cook, tossing, for 3-4 minutes or until heated. Season to taste with black pepper and serve immediately topped with Parmesan cheese.

Serves 4

This delicious combination of vegetables and prosciutto takes next to no time to prepare and is one of those wonderful one-dish meals. You might like to serve it with crusty French bread or wholemeal rolls.

PARSLEY BRAINS

4 sets lamb's brains
30 g/1 oz butter
2 tablespoons flour
1 cup/250 mL/8 fl oz milk
2 tablespoons chopped fresh parsley
freshly ground black pepper

1   Place brains in a bowl, cover with cold water and set aside to stand for 1 hour. Drain and peel membrane from brains. Place in a saucepan, cover with fresh cold water and bring to the boil. Reduce heat and simmer, uncovered, for 4 minutes. Drain and set aside.

2   Melt butter in a saucepan and cook flour for 1 minute. Gradually stir in milk and bring to the boil. Boil, stirring constantly, until sauce thickens. Stir in parsley and season to taste with black pepper.

3   Add brains to sauce and cook over a medium heat for 3-4 minutes or until heated through.

Serves 4

One of the traditional ways to serve lamb's brains. Accompany this dish with boiled, steamed or microwaved baby potatoes and a green vegetable such as beans.

Gnocchi with Herb Sauce

750 g/1¹/₂ lb gnocchi

FRESH HERB SAUCE
4 tablespoons chopped fresh parsley
4 tablespoons chopped fresh coriander
4 tablespoons chopped fresh basil
2 tablespoons pine nuts
1 tablespoon grated Parmesan cheese
1 tablespoon mayonnaise
1 tablespoon chicken stock
freshly ground black pepper

1   Cook gnocchi in boiling water in a large saucepan following packet directions. Drain, set aside and keep warm.

2   To make sauce, place parsley, coriander, basil, pine nuts and Parmesan cheese in a food processor or blender and process to combine. Add mayonnaise and stock and process to combine. Season to taste with black pepper. Spoon sauce over gnocchi and serve immediately.

For a complete meal, accompany with a tossed green salad and wholemeal bread rolls.

Gnocchi with Herb Sauce

Serves 4

Cheesy Herb Soufflé

CHEESY HERB SOUFFLE

45 g/1¹/₂ oz butter
¹/₄ cup/30 g/1 oz flour
1 cup/250 mL/8 fl oz milk
155 g/5 oz grated tasty cheese
(mature Cheddar)
75 g/2¹/₂ oz grated Parmesan cheese
¹/₄ teaspoon ground nutmeg
4 tablespoons chopped fresh parsley
4 tablespoons snipped fresh chives
1 tablespoon finely chopped fresh basil
1 tablespoon chopped fresh coriander
freshly ground black pepper
4 eggs, separated

Serves 4

1   Melt butter in a large saucepan and cook flour over a medium heat for 1 minute. Gradually stir in milk and cook, stirring constantly, until sauce is thick and smooth.

2   Stir in tasty cheese (mature Cheddar), Parmesan cheese, nutmeg, parsley, chives, basil, coriander and black pepper to taste, then beat in egg yolks one at a time.

3   Place egg whites in a clean bowl and beat until soft peaks form. Fold 2 tablespoons cheese mixture into egg whites, then fold egg white mixture into remaining cheese mixture.

4   Spoon soufflé mixture into a lightly greased 4-cup/1 litre/1³/₄ pint capacity soufflé dish and bake for 25-30 minutes or until soufflé is puffed and golden. Serve immediately.

Oven temperature
200°C, 400°F, Gas 6

The secrets to successful soufflé-making are to make sure that the oven is at the correct temperature, the basic mixture is ready, and the soufflé dish is prepared before you beat the egg whites.

Quick Calamari and Mint

3 tablespoons olive oil
2 cloves garlic, crushed
1/4 teaspoon chilli paste (sambal oelek)
3/4 cup/185 mL/6 fl oz tomato purée
1/4 cup/60 mL/2 fl oz dry white wine
500 g/1 lb calamari (squid) rings
1 tablespoon chopped fresh mint
freshly ground black pepper

1   Heat oil in a large saucepan and cook garlic, chilli paste (sambal oelek), tomato purée and wine over a medium heat for 3 minutes.

2   Add calamari (squid) rings and cook, stirring constantly, for 2 minutes or until calamari (squid) is just tender. Stir in mint and season to taste with black pepper. Serve immediately.

Serves 4

Remember that the cooking time for calamari (squid) should be either very short, just a few minutes, or very long, an hour or more gentle cooking, otherwise it will be tough.

Dill and Seafood Ragout

60 g/2 oz butter
2 onions, sliced
2 parsnips, sliced
4 cups/1 litre/1 3/4 pt chicken
or fish stock
1 cup/250 mL/8 fl oz white wine
1/4 cup/60 mL/2 fl oz lime or lemon juice
375 g/12 oz firm white fish fillets,
cut into chunks
375 g/12 oz mussels, in shell, scrubbed
and debearded
4 tablespoons sour cream
freshly ground black pepper
2 tablespoons chopped fresh dill

1   Melt butter in a large saucepan and cook onions and parsnips over a medium heat for 4-5 minutes or until onions are soft. Stir in stock, wine, lime or lemon juice, fish and mussels and cook for 4-5 minutes or until mussels open.

2   Using a slotted spoon, remove vegetables, fish and mussels from liquid. Discard any mussels that have not opened and remove meat from remaining mussel shells.

3   Stir sour cream into stock mixture, bring to simmering and simmer for 15-20 minutes or until reduced by half and sauce begins to thicken.

4   Return vegetables, fish and mussels to sauce, stir in dill, season to taste with black pepper and cook for 2 minutes. Serve immediately.

Serves 4

Dill is considered to be a herb of good omen. In some European countries, brides would place a sprig of dill and some salt in their shoes, as well as pinning a sprig to their dress.

38

*Quick Calamari and Mint,
Dill and Seafood Ragout*

Chive and Cheese Croquettes

CHIVE AND CHEESE CROQUETTES

500 g/1 lb mozzarella cheese, grated
1¹/₂ cups/185 g/6 oz flour
2 eggs, lightly beaten
4 tablespoons snipped fresh chives
¹/₂ teaspoon cayenne pepper
¹/₂ cup/60 g/2 oz cornflour
oil for deep-frying

1   Place mozzarella cheese, 1 cup/125 g/ 4 oz flour, eggs, chives and cayenne pepper in a bowl and mix to combine. Shape mixture into balls and place on a plate lined with plastic food wrap. Refrigerate for 30 minutes.

2   Combine cornflour and remaining flour and place on a plate. Roll balls in flour mixture and refrigerate for 10 minutes longer.

3   Heat oil in a deep saucepan and cook 4-5 croquettes at a time until golden. Remove, using a slotted spoon, drain on absorbent kitchen paper and serve immediately.

Makes 24

Croquettes can be prepared in advance and stored, covered, in the refrigerator until you are ready to cook them. The secret to good croquettes is to make sure that they are well chilled before cooking.

Tabbouleh Tomatoes

4 large tomatoes

TABBOULEH FILLING
3 tablespoons burghul (cracked wheat)
boiling water
8 spring onions, finely chopped
3 cloves garlic, crushed
3 tablespoons chopped fresh parsley
2 tablespoons chopped fresh mint
1 tablespoon olive oil
freshly ground black pepper

1 Using a sharp knife, cut tops from tomatoes, then scoop out flesh using a teaspoon. Chop flesh and reserve.

2 To make filling, place burghul (cracked wheat) in a bowl and pour over boiling water to cover. Set aside to soak for 10 minutes. Drain burghul (cracked wheat) and place in a bowl with tomato flesh, spring onions, garlic, parsley, mint, oil and black pepper to taste. Spoon filling into tomato shells and place on a baking tray. Bake for 10 minutes or until heated through.

Serves 4

Oven temperature
200°C, 400°F, Gas 6

Tabbouleh is a popular parsley salad originating from the Middle East. This filling is just as good served cold as a salad or as part of a sandwich filling.

Tabbouleh Tomatoes

CORIANDER BEEF PITTAS

500 g/1 lb rump steak, in one piece,
trimmed of all visible fat
2 cloves garlic, crushed
$^1/_3$ cup/90 mL/3 fl oz red wine
$^1/_4$ cup/60 mL/2 fl oz olive oil
freshly ground black pepper
3 tablespoons chopped fresh coriander
4 large pitta bread rounds, cut in half

CORIANDER HOLLANDAISE
2 cloves garlic
2 egg yolks
1 tablespoon lemon juice
2 tablespoons chopped fresh coriander
1 tablespoon chopped fresh parsley
125 g/4 oz butter
freshly ground black pepper

Of Middle Eastern origin, pitta bread makes a wonderful container for any type of filling. The Coriander Hollandaise used in this recipe is also delicious served with baked fish, or you might prefer to make this recipe using fish in place of the beef. If using fish, use white wine in place of the red wine and steam, bake or microwave the fish until it flakes when tested with a fork.

Coriander Beef Pittas

1   Place steak in a shallow dish. Place garlic, wine, oil and black pepper to taste in a bowl and mix well to combine. Pour over steak, cover and set aside to marinate for 30 minutes. Drain steak and cook under a preheated grill or on a preheated barbecue for 3-4 minutes each side or until cooked to your liking.

2   Slice steak diagonally across the grain and place in a bowl with coriander. Toss to combine. Fill pitta breads with steak mixture.

3   To make hollandaise, place garlic, egg yolks, lemon juice, coriander and parsley in a food processor or blender and process to combine. Melt butter until hot and bubbling. With machine running, slowly pour in melted butter and process until thick. Season to taste with black pepper, then spoon over meat and serve immediately.

Serves 4

LEEK AND DILL TART

315 g/10 oz prepared shortcrust pastry

LEEK FILLING
15 g/^{1}/$_2$ oz butter
4 small leeks, trimmed and thinly sliced
1 cup/200 g/6^1/$_2$ oz natural yogurt
1 tablespoon flour
2 eggs, lightly beaten
90 g/3 oz grated tasty cheese
(mature Cheddar)
3 tablespoons chopped fresh dill
freshly ground black pepper

1   Roll out pastry to line a lightly greased 20 cm/8 in loose-bottom flan tin. Prick base several times with a fork, line with nonstick baking paper and fill with uncooked rice. Bake for 8-10 minutes, remove rice and paper and bake for 5 minutes longer or until pastry is golden. Set aside to cool.

2   To make filling, melt butter in a frying pan and cook leeks for 4-5 minutes or until just tender.

3   Place yogurt, flour, eggs, three-quarters of the cheese and 1 tablespoon dill in a bowl and mix to combine. Fold in leeks, season to taste with black pepper and spoon into pastry case. Sprinkle with remaining cheese and dill and bake for 20 minutes or until tart is set.

Serves 4

Oven temperature
200°C, 400°F, Gas 6

Choose young thin leeks for this tart. The combination of young leeks and fresh dill gives the tart a garden-fresh taste.

Leek and Dill Tart

43

VEGETABLES

*Delicious, yet simple to make, these vegetables dishes –
all flavoured with herbs, of course – give new life to some
old favourites. Served on their own for a light meal, as part of a
vegetarian meal, or as an accompaniment to a meat dish, there
is sure to be something to suit all tastes and occasions.*

Rosemary Potato Bake

Ricotta and Herb
Vegetables

Coriander Bean Salad

Ratatouille

Golden Nugget Salad

Rosemary Sweet
Potatoes

Tomato Basil Salad

Pesto Potato Bake

Summer Vegetables
with Aioli

Rosemary Potato Bake

44

ROSEMARY POTATO BAKE

6 potatoes, thinly sliced
1 cup/250 mL/8 fl oz vegetable or
chicken stock
2 large leeks, white part only, sliced
2 cloves garlic, crushed
1 tablespoon finely chopped fresh
rosemary or 1 teaspoon dried rosemary
$^{1}/_{2}$ cup/30 g/1 oz bread crumbs, made
from stale bread
30 g/1 oz butter, melted
freshly ground black pepper

1   Boil, steam or microwave potato slices
until just tender. Refresh under cold
running water and set aside.

2   Place stock, leeks, garlic and rosemary
in a saucepan, bring to the boil, then
reduce heat and simmer for 3 minutes.

3   Arrange potato slices in layers in a
lightly greased ovenproof dish, and top
with leek mixture. Place bread crumbs,
butter and black pepper to taste in a bowl
and mix to combine. Sprinkle over leek
mixture and bake for 25-30 minutes.

Serves 4

Oven temperature
180°C, 350°F, Gas 4

Serve this potato dish as an
accompaniment to grilled
steak, chops or chicken.
For a vegetarian meal,
team it with a salad of
mixed lettuces, cucumber,
chopped parsley, spring
onions and grated
Parmesan cheese.

RICOTTA AND HERB VEGETABLES

prepared vegetables of your choice for
filling: zucchini (courgettes), red, green
or yellow peppers, eggplant (aubergines)
or baby pumpkins are all suitable

HERB FILLING
$^{1}/_{2}$ cup/30 g/1 oz bread crumbs, made
from stale bread
60 g/2 oz grated mozzarella cheese
125 g/4 oz ricotta cheese
3 tablespoons grated Parmesan cheese
1 tablespoon chopped fresh basil or
1 teaspoon dried basil
2 teaspoons chopped fresh oregano or
$^{1}/_{2}$ teaspoon dried oregano
1 egg white, lightly beaten
freshly ground black pepper

1   Boil, steam or microwave vegetable of
your choice until just tender. Drain and
refresh under cold running water. If you
have not removed the centre of the
vegetable before cooking, scoop it out
now and set the vegetable shells aside.

2   To make filling, place bread crumbs,
mozzarella cheese, ricotta cheese,
Parmesan cheese, basil and oregano in a
bowl and mix to combine. Stir in egg
white and black pepper to taste and mix
well. Use to fill vegetable shells. Place
vegetables in a lightly greased baking dish
and bake for 15 minutes or until filling is
heated and top browns.

Serves 4-6

Oven temperature
240°C, 475°F, Gas 8

It is difficult to give an exact
serving size for this recipe
as it depends on the
vegetable you choose. As a
guide, however, there is
enough filling for 6 large
zucchini (courgettes), or 4
red, green or yellow peppers,
or 2 baby pumpkins, or 4
eggplant (aubergines).

CORIANDER BEAN SALAD

All parts of the coriander plant can be used. However you should be aware that if a recipe calls for fresh coriander you should not substitute it for the dried seeds or ground coriander (this is ground coriander seeds not leaf), as the two have completely different flavours.

500 g/1 lb shelled fresh broad beans or frozen broad beans
250 g/8 oz fresh or frozen sweet corn kernels
4 tomatoes, cut into wedges
6 spring onions, chopped
2 tablespoons chopped fresh coriander

CUMIN DRESSING
1/4 cup/60 mL/2 fl oz olive oil
1/4 cup/60 mL/2 fl oz lemon juice
1/2 teaspoon ground cumin
freshly ground black pepper

1 Boil, steam or microwave broad beans and sweet corn, separately, until tender. Place hot broad beans, sweet corn, tomatoes, spring onions and coriander in a bowl.

2 To make dressing, place oil, lemon juice, cumin and black pepper to taste in a screwtop jar and shake well to combine. Pour over bean mixture and toss to combine. Set aside, tossing occasionally, until beans are cool.

Serves 8

RATATOUILLE

Ratatouille is delicious as a filling for red or green peppers. These are great as the main course of a vegetarian meal.
To complete the meal, accompany the filled peppers with crusty French bread and a tossed green salad.

2 eggplant (aubergines), cut into strips
salt
2 tablespoons olive oil
2 large red onions, sliced
2 cloves garlic, crushed
2 green peppers, sliced
440 g/14 oz canned tomatoes, undrained and mashed
4 tablespoons dry white wine
1 tablespoon chopped fresh oregano or 1 teaspoon dried oregano
1 tablespoon tomato paste (purée)
250 g/8 oz mushrooms, sliced
3 tablespoons chopped fresh parsley
freshly ground black pepper

1 Place eggplant (aubergines) in a colander set over a bowl and sprinkle with salt. Set aside to stand for 30 minutes, then rinse under cold running water and pat dry with absorbent kitchen paper.

2 Heat oil in a large frying pan and cook onions, garlic and green peppers over a medium heat for 3-4 minutes or until onions are soft. Add eggplant (aubergines), tomatoes, wine, oregano and tomato paste (purée) and cook, stirring, over a medium heat for 25-30 minutes or until mixture reduces and thickens. Stir in mushrooms and cook for 5 minutes longer. Add parsley and season to taste with black pepper. Serve hot, warm or at room temperature.

Serves 6

Coriander Bean Salad,
Ratatouille

Golden Nugget Salad

GOLDEN NUGGET SALAD

1 golden nugget or small pumpkin, cut
into thin wedges and seeds removed
220 g/7 oz snow peas (mangetout)
220 g/7 oz baby squash or
zucchini (courgettes)

DILL DRESSING
1 tablespoon chopped fresh dill
2 tablespoons lemon juice
$^1/_4$ cup/60 mL/2 fl oz olive oil
freshly ground black pepper

1   Boil, steam or microwave pumpkin,
snow peas (mangetout) and squash or
zucchini (courgettes) separately until just
tender. Drain, refresh under cold running
water and drain again. Place all
vegetables in a large bowl.

2   To make dressing, place dill, lemon
juice, oil and black pepper to taste in a
screwtop jar and shake well to combine.
Pour over vegetables and toss to combine.

Serves 4

A salad of wonderful colours.
You can use carrot instead of
the pumpkin if you wish.

ROSEMARY SWEET POTATOES

2 sweet potatoes, cut into thick slices
1 tablespoon finely chopped
fresh rosemary
2 cloves garlic, crushed
¹/4 cup/60 mL/2 fl oz olive oil
freshly ground black pepper

Serves 4

1   Layer sweet potato slices in a lightly greased ovenproof dish and sprinkle with rosemary.

2   Combine garlic and olive oil, drizzle over sweet potatoes and season to taste with black pepper. Bake for 30 minutes or until sweet potatoes are tender.

Oven temperature
180°C, 350°F, Gas 4

TOMATO BASIL SALAD

2 large tomatoes, sliced
60 g/2 oz fresh basil leaves
1 red onion, sliced into rings

GARLIC DRESSING
2 cloves garlic, crushed
2 teaspoons olive oil
1 tablespoon lime or lemon juice
freshly ground black pepper

1   Cut each tomato slice in half and arrange alternately with basil leaves on a large serving platter. Place onion rings in centre of platter.

2   To make dressing, place garlic, oil, lime or lemon juice and black pepper to taste in a screwtop jar and shake well to combine. Drizzle over salad.

Serves 4

Ever popular as an accompaniment to barbecued or grilled food, this salad adds colour and flavour to any meal. Use fresh young basil leaves, or you might like to use mint leaves to create a Tomato Mint Salad – delicious with grilled or barbecued lamb chops.

Tomato Basil Salad

PESTO POTATO BAKE

Oven temperature
180°C, 350°F, Gas 4

The Pesto used in this recipe is also delicious tossed through pasta or boiled, steamed or microwaved vegetables such as squash or carrots.

8 potatoes, thickly sliced

PESTO
60 g/2 oz basil leaves
2 cloves garlic, crushed
2 tablespoons pine nuts
$^{1}/_{2}$ cup/125 mL/4 fl oz olive oil
4 tablespoons grated Parmesan cheese

SOUR CREAM TOPPING
300 g/9$^{1}/_{2}$ oz sour cream
60 g/2 oz grated tasty cheese
(mature Cheddar)
freshly ground black pepper

1   Boil, steam or microwave potato slices until almost tender. Drain, then layer in the base of a lightly greased ovenproof dish.

2   To make Pesto, place basil, garlic, pine nuts, oil and Parmesan cheese in a food processor or blender and process until smooth. Spread over potatoes.

3   To make topping, spoon sour cream over Pesto and top with tasty cheese (mature Cheddar) and black pepper to taste. Bake for 10 minutes or until potatoes are tender and top is golden brown.

Pesto Potato Bake

Serves 4

Summer Vegetables with Aioli

SUMMER VEGETABLES WITH AIOLI

250 g/8 oz asparagus, trimmed
12 yellow baby squash or
zucchini (courgettes)
125 g/4 oz green beans, trimmed
12 baby potatoes
12 button mushrooms
12 cherry tomatoes

PARSLEY AIOLI
4 egg yolks
2 teaspoons lemon juice
4 cloves garlic
2 tablespoons chopped fresh parsley
1 cup/250 mL/8 fl oz olive oil
freshly ground black pepper

1   Boil, steam or microwave asparagus, squash or zucchini (courgettes), beans and potatoes, separately, until just tender. Drain, then refresh under cold running water.

2   To make aioli, place egg yolks, lemon juice, garlic and parsley in a food processor or blender and process to combine. With machine running, pour in oil in a steady stream and process until thick. Transfer to a serving bowl.

3   Arrange asparagus, squash or zucchini (courgettes), beans, potatoes, mushrooms and tomatoes attractively on a large platter with aioli.

Serves 12

Raw garlic has a strong taste and can leave you with 'garlic breath'. If you find this a problem, you might like to boil the garlic cloves (in their skin) before using. Garlic treated in this way has a milder flavour, which is preferred by some people, and will not linger as strongly on the breath. To sweeten your breath after eating garlic, munch on some parsley.

51

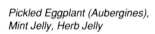

PRESERVES

Flavour your preserves with herbs. A basic apple jelly is easily turned into delicious Herb Jelly with the addition of chopped fresh herbs. A flourishing mint plant gives you the opportunity to make wonderful Mint Chutney. If you have never ventured into preserving, why not start by trying some of these mouthwatering recipes.

MINT JELLY

3 kg/6 lb cooking apples, quartered
juice 4 lemons
125 g/4 oz fresh mint leaves
water
1 cup/250 mL/8 fl oz white wine vinegar
sugar
chopped fresh mint leaves
green food colouring

1 Place apples, lemon juice and mint in a large saucepan with just enough water to cover. Bring to simmering and simmer until apples are very soft. Stir in vinegar, bring back to simmering and simmer for 5 minutes longer.

2 Strain mixture through a jelly bag, then measure juices and allow 220 g/7 oz sugar for each 1 cup/250 mL/8 fl oz of juice.

3 Place juice and sugar in a clean, large saucepan and cook over a low heat, stirring, until sugar dissolves. Increase heat and boil rapidly for 5 minutes or until jelly reaches 105°C/221°F on a sugar thermometer. Stir in mint, and tint with a little food colouring. Skim scum from top of jelly and ladle into hot, sterilised jars. Wipe rims of jars using a clean, damp cloth and cover.

Makes 4 x 250 g/8 oz jars

Pickled Eggplant (Aubergines), Mint Jelly, Herb Jelly

HERB JELLY

1.5 kg/3 lb cooking apples,
coarsely chopped
6 cups/1.5 litres/2^1/$_2$ pt water
1^1/$_4$ cups/315 mL/10 fl oz white vinegar
sugar
30 g/1 oz chopped fresh tarragon,
parsley, basil or mint
red food colouring (optional)

1   Place apples, water and vinegar in a large saucepan, bring to simmering and simmer until apples are very soft. Strain mixture through a jelly bag, then measure juices and allow 500 g/1 lb sugar for each 2^1/$_2$ cups/600 mL/1 pt of juice.

2   Place juice in a clean, large saucepan and cook over a low heat. Add sugar and stir until sugar dissolves. Increase heat and boil rapidly for 10-15 minutes or until jelly reaches 105°C/221°F on a sugar thermometer.

3   Remove pan from heat and stir in tarragon, parsley, basil or mint. Tint with a little food colouring if desired. Skim scum from top of jelly and ladle into hot, sterilised jars. Wipe rims of jars using a clean, damp cloth and cover.

Makes 2 x 250 g/8 oz jars

Always use clean, unchipped jars for storing your preserves. Jars should be warm when adding the hot preserve, as cold jars will crack or break if a hot mixture is suddenly added to them.

PICKLED EGGPLANT (AUBERGINES)

2 kg/4 lb eggplant (aubergines), peeled
and cut into strips
4 tablespoons salt
4 cups/1 litre/1^3/$_4$ pt white wine vinegar
2 tablespoons sugar
^{1}/$_2$ cup/125 mL/4 fl oz olive oil
3 tablespoons snipped fresh chives
2 tablespoons chopped fresh marjoram
or oregano
4 small dried chillies
8 cloves garlic, peeled and halved

1   Place eggplant (aubergines) in a colander set over a bowl and sprinkle with salt. Set aside to stand for 30 minutes. Rinse eggplant (aubergines) under cold running water and set aside.

2   Place vinegar and sugar in a large saucepan and bring to the boil. Add eggplant (aubergines), return mixture to the boil, then reduce heat and simmer for 5 minutes. Drain eggplant (aubergines) and reserve liquid.

3   Combine hot eggplant (aubergines), oil, chives and marjoram or oregano and pack into hot, sterilised jars. Add 1 chilli and 4 garlic halves to each jar, then, using a wooden spoon, press down eggplant (aubergines) and top up jars with reserved liquid. Wipe rims of jars with a clean, damp cloth and cover. Store for 1 month before using.

Makes 4 x 500 g/1 lb jars

To sterilise jars, wash in hot water then warm in the oven at a low temperature until dry. Remember that the lids must also be sterilised.

MINT CHUTNEY

2.5 kg/5 lb cooking apples, peeled, cored
and finely chopped
2 cups/500 g/1 lb demerara or
muscovado sugar
2$\frac{1}{2}$ cups/600 mL/1 pt cider vinegar
250 g/8 oz onions, chopped
250 g/8 oz pitted dates, chopped
250 g/8 oz sultanas
1 tablespoon salt
1 tablespoon ground ginger
4 tablespoons chopped fresh mint

1   Place apples, sugar, vinegar, onions,
dates, sultanas, salt and ginger in a large
saucepan and, stirring, bring to the boil.
Reduce heat and simmer, stirring
frequently, for 1-1$\frac{1}{4}$ hours or until
chutney is thick. Stir in mint.

2   Pack chutney into hot, sterilised
jars, wipe rims of jars with a clean, damp
cloth and cover. Store for 1 month
before using.

Makes 6 x 500 g/1 lb jars

Mint Chutney

Preserves make wonderful
gifts. Save attractive jars and
use for your preserves. The
lids can be covered with
fabric covers and tied with
pretty ribbons. Remember to
label the jars and, if you are
giving an unusual jelly,
chutney or relish, it is often a
good idea to suggest what
to serve it with.

ROSEMARY QUINCE JELLY

3 kg/6 lb quinces, coarsely chopped
juice 3 lemons
sugar
3 tablespoons finely chopped fresh
rosemary
sprigs fresh rosemary

If quinces are unavailable,
apples can be used instead
to make an Apple and
Rosemary Jelly. Either jelly is
delicious served with hot or
cold roast lamb, grilled lamb
chops or with a sharp
Cheddar cheese.

1   Place quinces, lemon juice and
rosemary in a large saucepan with just
enough water to cover. Bring to
simmering and simmer until quinces are
very soft.

2   Strain mixture through a jelly bag,
then measure juices and allow 220 g/7 oz
sugar for each 1 cup/250 mL/8 fl oz
of juice.

3   Place juice and sugar in a clean, large
saucepan and cook over a low heat,
stirring, until sugar dissolves. Increase
heat and boil rapidly for 5 minutes or
until jelly reaches 105°C/221°F on a sugar
thermometer. Place a sprig of rosemary in
hot, sterilised jars. Skim scum from top of
jelly and ladle into jars. Wipe rims of jars
using a clean, damp cloth and cover.

Makes 6 x 250 g/8 oz jars

DILL PICKLES

3.5 kg/7 lb pickling cucumbers
boiling water
4 cups/1 litre/1^3/4 pt cider vinegar
8 cups/2 kg/4 lb sugar
2 tablespoons cooking salt
2 tablespoons mixed pickling spice
2 tablespoons dill seed

Makes 10 x 500 g/1 lb jars

1   Place cucumbers in a large bowl and cover with boiling water. Cover and set aside to stand for 24 hours. Drain, then repeat process three more times.

2   Place vinegar, sugar, salt and pickling spice in a large saucepan and bring to the boil. Pour over drained cucumbers, cover and set aside to stand for 24 hours. Drain and reserve liquid.

3   Bring reserved vinegar liquid to the boil, add cucumbers and bring back to the boil. Pack hot cucumbers into hot, sterilised jars, add dill seed and pour over boiling liquid. Wipe rims of jars with a clean, damp cloth and cover. Store for 2 weeks before using.

Preserves should be covered either immediately after potting or when completely cold. Never cover when just warm, as this creates conditions ideal for the growth of mould. If you are going to allow the preserve to cool before covering, place a clean cloth over the jars to prevent dust falling on the surface.

Rosemary Quince Jelly

BAKED GOODS

*Savoury baked goods are often flavoured with
herbs – in fact herbs and cheese are a favourite combination.
This selection of recipes includes chive-flavoured biscuits –
perfect with pre-dinner drinks; individual pizzas – just
the thing to feed hungry teenagers; and low-fat oat
scones with herbs for the health-conscious.*

Chive and Cheese
Biscuits

Pesto Pinwheels

Herb Oat Scones

Crispy Wholemeal
Pizza

Individual Herb Pizzas

Mixed Herb Muffins

Chive and Cheese Biscuits

CHIVE AND CHEESE BISCUITS

1 cup/125 g/4 oz self-raising flour, sifted
125 g/4 oz butter
60 g/2 oz blue cheese
2 tablespoons grated Parmesan cheese
3 tablespoons snipped fresh chives
4 tablespoons sesame seeds

Makes 30

1　Place flour, butter, blue cheese, Parmesan cheese and chives in a food processor and process until ingredients cling together. Turn onto a lightly floured surface and knead lightly. Wrap in plastic food wrap and refrigerate for 30 minutes.

2　Roll teaspoonfuls of mixture into balls, then roll in sesame seeds. Place on lightly greased baking trays, press with a fork and bake for 10 minutes or until golden. Stand on trays for 3 minutes before removing to wire racks to cool completely.

Oven temperature
180°C, 350°F, Gas 4

These savoury biscuits keep well in an airtight container and are a great standby when unexpected guests drop in.

PESTO PINWHEELS

2 cups/250 g/8 oz self-raising flour
1 teaspoon baking powder
2 teaspoons sugar
45 g/1^1/2 oz butter
1 egg, lightly beaten
^{3}/4 cup/185 mL/6 fl oz milk
60 g/2 oz grated tasty cheese
(mature Cheddar)

PESTO FILLING
90 g/3 oz fresh basil leaves
3 cloves garlic, crushed
3 tablespoons pine nuts, toasted
3 tablespoons olive oil
3 tablespoons grated Parmesan cheese
freshly ground black pepper

1　To make filling, place basil, garlic, pine nuts and 2 tablespoons oil in a food processor or blender and process until combined. With machine running, gradually add remaining oil. Transfer to a small bowl and mix in Parmesan cheese and black pepper to taste.

2　Sift flour and baking powder together into a bowl, then mix in sugar. Rub in butter, using your fingertips, until mixture resembles fine bread crumbs. Make a well in the centre of the flour and, using a round-ended knife, mix egg and ^{1}/2 cup/125 mL/4 fl oz milk into the flour mixture. Mix to a soft dough, adding a little more milk if necessary.

3　Turn dough onto a lightly floured surface and knead with fingertips until smooth. Roll out dough to form a rectangle 1 cm/^{1}/2 in thick. Spread with filling and roll up like a Swiss roll. Cut into 2 cm/^{3}/4 in slices and place on a lightly greased and floured baking tray. Brush with remaining milk and sprinkle with tasty cheese (mature Cheddar). Bake for 15-20 minutes or until scones are cooked.

Makes 10

Oven temperature
220°C, 425°F, Gas 7

These delicious pinwheels require no buttering and are best served warm or straight from the oven. As a morning tea or lunch treat, they are sure to be popular.

Herb Oat Scones

HERB OAT SCONES

Oven temperature
220°C, 425°F, Gas 7

1¹/₂ cups/185 g/6 oz self-raising
flour, sifted
¹/₂ cup/45 g/1¹/₂ oz instant oats
¹/₂ teaspoon baking powder
30 g/1 oz butter
2 teaspoons chopped fresh parsley
2 teaspoons chopped fresh basil
2 teaspoons chopped fresh rosemary or
¹/₂ teaspoon dried rosemary
³/₄ cup/185 mL/6 fl oz milk

1 Place flour, oats and baking powder in
a bowl. Rub in butter, using your fingertips,
until mixture resembles fine bread crumbs.
Stir in parsley, basil and rosemary.

2 Make a well in the centre of the flour
mixture and pour in milk. Mix lightly
with a round-ended blade knife until all
ingredients are just combined. Turn
mixture onto a lightly floured surface and
knead lightly.

3 Press dough out evenly to 2 cm/³/₄ in
thickness and cut into rounds using a
5 cm/2 in scone cutter dipped in flour.
Arrange scones side by side in a lightly
greased 18 cm/7 in round shallow cake
tin. Brush tops of scones with a little milk
and bake for 15-20 minutes or until scones
are golden.

For those on a low-
cholesterol diet, make
these scones using
polyunsaturated margarine
and skim milk. This cuts down
the fat content and the
scones will have virtually no
cholesterol.

Makes 9

CRISPY WHOLEMEAL PIZZA

Oven temperature
200°C, 400°F, Gas 6

PIZZA BASE

$^3/_4$ cup/125 g/4 oz wholemeal flour,
sifted and husks returned
$^3/_4$ cup/90 g/3 oz flour, sifted
1 teaspoon sugar
7 g/$^1/_4$ oz active dry yeast
$^1/_2$ cup/125 mL/4 fl oz warm water
4 tablespoons olive or vegetable oil

TOPPING

2 tablespoons olive or vegetable oil
2 onions, chopped
2 cloves garlic, crushed
440 g/14 oz canned tomatoes, undrained
and mashed
1 tablespoon chopped fresh basil
2 small red chillies, seeds removed
and chopped
1 green pepper, sliced
350 g/11 oz canned unsweetened
pineapple pieces, drained
6 stuffed olives, sliced
250 g/8 oz grated mozzarella cheese

Serves 6

1   To make base, place wholemeal flour, flour, sugar and yeast in a large mixing bowl. Make a well in the centre, add water and oil and mix to a soft dough. Turn dough onto a lightly floured surface and knead for 10 minutes. Place dough in a lightly oiled bowl, cover with plastic food wrap and set aside in a warm place to rise for 30 minutes or until dough has doubled in size. Punch dough down and knead on a lightly floured surface until smooth. Roll out to fit a lightly greased 30 cm/12 in pizza tray.

2   For topping, heat oil in a large frying pan and cook onions and garlic for 4-5 minutes or until onions are soft. Add tomatoes, basil and chillies and simmer, uncovered, for 15-20 minutes or until mixture reduces and thickens. Spread tomato sauce over pizza base, then top with green pepper, pineapple and olives, and sprinkle with mozzarella cheese. Bake for 20 minutes or until base is crispy and golden.

Crispy Wholemeal Pizza

INDIVIDUAL HERB PIZZAS

Oven temperature
200°C, 400°F, Gas 6

The dough for these pizzas takes very little time to make, is easy to handle, and can be made in advance and stored in the refrigerator. Bring back to room temperature before using. If some of the oil separates during storage, knead the dough to incorporate the oil again before using.

Individual Herb Pizzas

PIZZA DOUGH
4¹/₂ cups/560 g/1 lb 2 oz flour
3 tablespoons caster sugar
1 teaspoon salt
2 eggs, lightly beaten
1 cup/250 mL/8 fl oz olive oil
¹/₃ cup/90 mL/3 fl oz dry white wine

HERB TOPPING
4 tablespoons tomato paste (purée)
1 onion, thinly sliced
2 tomatoes, thinly sliced
1 tablespoon dried oregano
freshly ground black pepper

Makes 8 individual pizzas

1 To make dough, place flour, sugar and salt in a food processor and pulse once or twice to mix. With machine running, add eggs, then slowly pour in oil and wine. Continue processing until a smooth, glossy ball forms. Turn onto a lightly floured surface and knead briefly. Place in a bowl, cover and refrigerate until ready to use.

2 Divide dough into eight portions and roll each portion out to a 15 cm/ 6 in round.

3 To top pizza, spread each round with tomato paste (purée), then top with onion rings and tomato slices and sprinkle with oregano and black pepper to taste. Bake for 10-15 minutes or until dough is crisp and golden.

MIXED HERB MUFFINS

2 cups/250 g/8 oz flour, sifted
2 tablespoons sugar
3 teaspoons baking powder
1 egg
$^1/_2$ cup/125 mL/4 fl oz milk
30 g/1 oz butter, melted
60 g/2 oz chopped mixed fresh herbs,
such as parsley, thyme, oregano and sage

1   Sift flour, sugar and baking powder together into a mixing bowl. Make a well in the centre of the flour mixture and add egg, milk and butter. Mix to combine, then stir in herbs.

2   Spoon batter into lightly greased muffin pans and bake for 15-20 minutes or until muffins are cooked when tested with a skewer. Turn onto a wire rack to cool.

Makes 12

Oven temperature
190°C, 375°F, Gas 5

Mixed Herb Muffins

Muffins are becoming increasingly popular as an alternative to bread for breakfast, lunch – or just for snacking. These muffins make a tasty alternative to the many sweet ones offered. They freeze well, so make a batch and pop them in the freezer to have on hand for a delicious treat.

PRESERVING HERBS

There are several ways in which herbs can be preserved. Probably the most common is drying, but freezing is also successful and, of course, vinegars, oils, butters and pastes, or sauces such as Pesto also preserve the wonderful flavour of herbs for year-round use.

The flavour of dried herbs is very concentrated, so you need to use less than fresh herbs when cooking. Generally speaking, use about one-third of the amount of dried herbs as you would fresh herbs.

DRYING HERBS

Some of the most successful herbs to dry are marjoram, oregano, sage, mint, bay leaves, thyme and rosemary. The leafy herbs, such as basil, parsley, dill and chives, tend to lose much of their flavour and colour on drying.

To dry herbs is inexpensive and easy. The simplest method is to tie the herbs in small loose bunches and to hang them upside down in an airy place. The bunches must be small or the air will not circulate through the herbs enough to dry the centre ones.

Herbs can also be dried by placing them, still on their stems, in a single layer on a muslin-covered rack. Place the rack in a dry, airy room and leave until herbs are dried. The length of time this will take depends on the herb. The more delicate herbs will take 1 to 3 days while the tougher herbs, such as thyme, oregano and rosemary, will take up to a week. Once dried, remove the leaves from the stems and place in airtight containers. Always store dried herbs in a cool dark place, as heat and light quickly deplete the volatile oils. Dried herbs are at their best within 6 months of drying; after this they tend to lose their flavour and eventually become stale.

Herbs can also be dried in the microwave oven. It is difficult to give an exact time for drying herbs in the microwave as this varies from herb to herb and on the amount of moisture in and on the herb at the time of drying. Drying herbs in the microwave, however, is very successful and quick. While many people recommend placing the herbs on absorbent kitchen paper, care does need to be taken that the paper does not ignite during the drying process.

To dry herbs in the microwave, place the herbs on a microwave-safe plate or on absorbent kitchen paper and microwave on HIGH (100%) for 30 seconds. Turn herbs over and microwave for 30 seconds longer. Continue in this way until herbs are dry. The green, leafy herbs, such as parsley and basil, tend to retain more of their colour and flavour when dried in this way as compared with conventional methods.

Most fresh herbs will keep for about a week if stored correctly. Store fresh herbs in the refrigerator in a sealed plastic food bag. Placing the herbs in a jar of water and covering with a plastic food bag, then sealing the bag around the jar is probably the method that will keep herbs fresh for the longest period of time. Remember to change the water regularly – every day is best – to keep the herbs as fresh as possible. Herbs such as basil and mint do not keep as well as parsley, coriander or chives.

FREEZING HERBS

If you grow your own herbs, use the freezer to preserve them. Frozen herbs are closest in flavour and colour to fresh herbs and are ideal to use in cooking. Herbs that freeze particularly well are chives, chervil, dill, fennel leaves, parsley and tarragon. During freezing, these leafy herbs tend to toughen slightly, go limp and darken and so are not suitable for garnishing, but are perfect for cooking. Use the same quantity of frozen herbs, as you would use fresh in cooking. There is no need to thaw, just add straight to the dish that you are cooking.

There are several ways of freezing herbs. The simplest method is to collect them in the early morning after the dew has dried; wash the herbs gently under cold running water and shake off excess water; place on absorbent kitchen paper and pat dry; then place in a freezer bag, seal, label and freeze.

Herbs can be frozen on the stem, as single leaves, sprigs, diced or chopped. It is best to tray-freeze stems, sprigs and leaves first. They do not stick together during freezing and are easy to use and remove for cooking. After preparation, place the herbs on a tray lined with aluminium foil or freezer wrap and freeze overnight, then pack into freezer bags or containers.

Diced or chopped herbs can be frozen in two ways: place the diced or chopped herbs straight into a freezer bag and freeze, then scoop out the required amount when needed; or place the chopped or diced herbs in an ice cube tray with a little stock or water, freeze and, when frozen, remove from tray and pack into freezer bags. Just add to the pot for instant flavour when required.

You might also like to consider freezing favourite combinations of herbs in ice cube form, so that only one or two cubes need to be added – make sure you know which is which by labelling them. Another way to preserve herbs is to freeze them in butter or oil.

Depending on the herb, either place single leaves or sprigs in a freezer bag, seal, label and freeze until required. The large-leaved herbs are best frozen as single leaves while the small-leaved ones are best as sprigs. Add the frozen herbs to soups, casseroles, sauces or marinades.

HERB VINEGARS

Flavoured vinegars give extra flavour to any savoury dish, pickle or salad and can be used in place of malt, white, cider or wine vinegar.

Allow 2 cups, about 125 g/4 oz, slightly crushed fresh herb leaves to each 4 cups/1 litre/1 $\frac{3}{4}$ pt cider or wine vinegar.

1 Wash herbs gently, shake and dry thoroughly by patting with absorbent kitchen paper.

2 Place herbs in sterilised jars.

For a stronger flavoured vinegar repeat the distilling and straining process.

3 Fill jars with wine or cider vinegar. Seal and leave for 1-2 weeks.

4 Strain liquid through a jelly bag or double thickness of muslin into attractive bottles. Discard herbs. Place a sprig or two of the herb used in each bottle and seal.

HERB OILS

Herb oils are delicious brushed on food before grilling, on barbecue grills, frying pans and baking dishes, or used in dressings, sauces and marinades. They are also easy to make – all they require is a little time to steep.

When making flavoured oils, choose a bland oil such as sunflower or safflower oil. Any oil can in fact be used, but it is best to avoid the strong-tasting ones.

Most herbs are suitable to use, but they should be fresh.

Herb oils and vinegars make inexpensive gifts and are always popular for fetes. They look wonderful when placed in attractive bottles with decorative labels.

You will need enough herbs to half fill a bottle or jar. Lightly bruise the herbs, place in the bottle or jar, then pour over enough oil to fill the jar. Seal and leave in a warm place, shaking each day, for 2 weeks. Strain the oil, pressing the herbs to extract the flavour, and taste and if it is not strong enough repeat the process. When the oil is the desired flavour, place in attractive bottles with a fresh sprig of the herb used. Seal and label.

A selection of Herb Vinegars and Herb Oils

FRENCH POTPOURRI

These recipes are only a guide to the types of potpourri you can make. Adapt them to use whatever flowers and herbs you have available. Always be cautious when adding essential oils.

4 cups dried red rose petals
1 cup dried lavender flowers
1 cup dried lemon peel
1 cup fixative
1 cup dried rosemary
1 cup dried thyme
1 cup dried sage
1 cup dried marjoram
2 tablespoons coriander seeds,
lightly crushed
rose oil
lavender oil

1   Place rose petals, lavender flowers, lemon peel and fixative in a large bowl and mix to combine. Add rosemary, thyme, sage, marjoram and coriander seeds and toss to mix thoroughly.

2   Add rose and lavender oils drop by drop, mixing potpourri well as you go.

3   Transfer to a large container, seal and set aside to mature for 6 weeks before using.

CITRUS POTPOURRI

Fixatives are essential to help fix and stabilise the overall perfumes of potpourri for a very long time. The most common fixative is orris root powder which slows the evaporation of the oils. When dried, orris root powder has a delicate violet scent. Other fixatives include gum benzoin, sandalwood and oakmoss. Dried citrus rinds such as orange and lemon peel are also good for fixing a scent. The rinds must be pared very thinly from the fruit to avoid leaving any pith attached, which can send the peel mouldy.

8 cups of a combination of any of the following: lemon verbena, lemon-scented tea tree, lemon thyme, lemon-scented geranium and/or lemon grass
1 cup fixative
1 cup eau-de-cologne mint
1 cup calendula petals
$1/2$ cup dried orange peel
$1/2$ cup dried lemon peel
1 cup whole allspice, lightly crushed
lemon verbena oil
bergamot oil

1   Place lemon-scented plants of your choice and fixative in a large bowl and mix to combine. Add mint, calendula petals, orange and lemon peel, and allspice and toss to mix thoroughly.

2   Add lemon verbena and bergamot oils drop by drop, mixing potpourri well as you go.

3   Transfer to a large container, seal and set aside to mature for 6 weeks before using.

COLLECTING HERBS AND FLOWERS

The following hints will ensure that you achieve the best possible results if collecting herbs and flowers for drying from your garden.

🍃 Pick only blemish-free petals, flowers, leaves and herbs. Pass over all petals that are rain-damaged.

🍃 Gather only on a fine day, preferably after a spell of dry weather.

🍃 Do not water the plants the day before harvesting.

🍃 Pick after the morning dew has dried, but before the sun is high.

🍃 Rose petals and small whole flowers such as violets should be spread out evenly on racks, shallow boxes or newspaper to dry.

🍃 Herbs, lavender and aromatic foliage can be tied in small loose bunches and hung to dry.

🍃 Flowers and herbs are best dried away from strong light and where the air can circulate around them.

🍃 As soon as the plant material is completely dry, store in separate, labelled glass containers with lids. Store in a dark, dry place.

🍃 Pick and dry plants as they come into flower and add newly dried petals to the jars.

Essential oils enhance the scent of most potpourri and sachet blends, but should be used very sparingly. Add one drop at a time, smelling and blending as you go. Fixatives and essential oils can be obtained from chemists or health food shops.

Ingredients for making potpourri

MINT SAUCE

1¹/₂-2 tablespoons caster sugar
15 g/¹/₂ oz fresh mint leaves
1 tablespoon boiling water
¹/₂ cup/125 mL/4 fl oz red wine
or malt vinegar

2 Finely chop mint and place in a bowl. Pour boiling water over and stir to dissolve sugar.

Mint Sauce is the traditional accompaniment for roast lamb.

1 Sprinkle sugar over mint leaves.

3 Set aside to cool, then stir in vinegar, cover and refrigerate until ready to use.

Makes ¹/₂ cup/125 mL/4 fl oz

Mint Sauce

SAGE AND ONION PINWHEELS

250 g/8 oz cream cheese
30 fresh sage leaves
3 tablespoons finely chopped
spring onions
freshly ground black pepper

1 Soften cream cheese and spread out on a 20 cm/8 in square sheet of aluminium foil.

2 Lay sage leaves evenly over the cheese, sprinkle with spring onions and season to taste with black pepper.

3 Using the foil as a guide, roll up the cheese, making a tight log. Chill for 1-2 hours or until firm. Just prior to serving, remove foil and cut roll into slices. Serve with crackers or Melba toast.

Makes 20 pinwheels

These pinwheels are also delicious made using chopped fresh parsley or basil instead of the sage.

Sage and Onion Pinwheels

HERB BUTTERS

BASIL BUTTER

Place 125 g/4 oz softened butter and 8-10 finely chopped basil leaves in a bowl and beat until creamy. Press into a butter mould or roll into a cylinder or balls, cover with plastic food wrap and refrigerate until firm.

MIXED HERB BUTTER

Place 125 g/4 oz softened butter in a bowl and beat until creamy. Add 1 teaspoon each of finely chopped parsley, sage, thyme and rosemary and beat again until herbs are evenly distributed through butter. Press into a butter mould or roll into a cylinder or balls, cover with plastic food wrap and refrigerate until firm.

Herb butters are a delicious alternative to ordinary butter on sandwiches. Try Basil Butter next time you make tomato sandwiches.

GARLIC BUTTER

Place 125 g/4 oz softened butter, 4 cloves of crushed garlic, $1/2$ teaspoon white pepper and 2 tablespoons finely chopped fresh parsley in a bowl and beat until creamy. Press into a butter mould or roll into a cylinder or balls, cover with plastic food wrap and refrigerate until firm.

A selection of Herb Butters

SAGE AND APPLE JELLY

3 kg/6 lb cooking apples, quartered
juice 4 lemons
1 cup/250 mL/8 fl oz white
wine vinegar
sugar
sprigs fresh sage

1   Place apples and lemon juice in a large saucepan with just enough water to cover apples. Bring to simmering and simmer until apples are very soft. Stir in vinegar, bring to the boil and boil for 5 minutes.

2   Strain mixture through a jelly bag or double thickness of muslin. Do not press the mixture as this causes the jelly to cloud. The straining process will take an hour or more. Measure juices and allow 220 g/7 oz sugar for each 1 cup/250 mL/8 fl oz of juice.

When making jelly, the whole fruit is used, so do not peel or core the apples.

3   Place juice and sugar in a clean, large saucepan and bring to the boil, stirring until sugar dissolves. Increase heat and boil rapidly for 10-15 minutes or until jelly reaches 105°C/221°F on a sugar thermometer.

4   Place sage sprigs in hot sterilised jars. Skim scum from top of jelly and ladle into jars. Wipe rims of jars using a clean, damp cloth and cover.

Makes 4 x 250 g/8 oz jars

Sage and Apple Jelly

AN A TO Z OF HERBS

ANGELICA

This is a stout biennial herb which grows to 2 m/6^{1}/2 ft or more. Leaves are soft green and divided into large leaflets. The stems are round, ribbed and hollow with yellow-green flowers which grow in a ball-like cluster. Angelica is best suited to cool-climate areas where it can be planted in sun or semi-shade. Shelter from strong wind is desirable because the stems are brittle. Angelica is completely permeated by a unique essence, giving it a delicately sweet and refreshing aroma. The stems can be used instead of sugar when stewing sour fruits such as rhubarb. The roots are edible and can be cooked, and served as a vegetable. The seeds are used as a flavouring in gin and some liqueurs.

BASIL

An annual that grows to 60 cm/2 ft high, basil has peppery, clove-scented leaves. There are many different types of basil, but sweet basil and bush basil are still the best varieties to grow for the kitchen. Grown from seed, basil requires a sunny, moist but well-drained position that is sheltered from wind. For best results, sow the seed at the end of spring or beginning of summer. To encourage longer life, remove the small, white flower buds as they appear. Basil loses much of its flavour when dried, so use fresh basil when a stronger taste is needed. Excellent with all tomato dishes and torn up in salads, it also goes well with carrots, zucchini (courgettes), pasta sauces and chicken.

BAY

This slow-growing evergreen tree, also known as bay laurel or sweet bay has aromatic leaves. Bay trees are excellent tub specimens and should be grown in a sunny, sheltered position. Young plants need protection from frosts. The leaves of the bay tree are large, flat, oval and glossy and can be harvested at any time of the year. Bay leaves have a strong flavour and taste, rather bitter when fresh, so are most often used dried. Use with tomatoes and beetroot and to flavour soups, sauces and stews. Added to flour and similar foods, bay leaves help to keep weevils away.

BORAGE

This herb is an annual with large leaves and thick, soft, branching hairy stems. Its height varies from 30-90 cm/1-3 ft and the leaves are greyish-green and 10-15 cm/4-6 in in length. The star-like summer flowers of either white or blue are most attractive and borage will continue to flower through winter in mild areas. Both the flowers and young leaves can be eaten. The leaves have a delicate, cucumber-like flavour and, finely chopped, they are a delicious salad garnish. The flowers can be candied.

CHERVIL

This is a small spreading annual that grows to 45 cm/1^{1}/2 ft. Its fern-like leaves have a delicate aniseed flavour and the white flowers, which appear in early summer, grow in small, flat umbels. The seeds of chervil resemble caraway seeds but are longer and thinner. The seeds should be sown in spring and autumn in shallow drills 30 cm/1 ft apart. Chervil should be grown in a partially shaded, sheltered position in a rich, moist soil. Chervil leaves are delicious with salad greens and spinach, in dressings, as a garnish for soups or with fish dishes.

CHIVES

A perennial member of the onion family, chives have hollow onion-flavoured leaves with attractive edible mauve flowers. Chives like a rich, moist soil in full sun and they also grow well indoors in

pots on a sunny windowsill. They respond to picking in moderation, but a proportion of fresh leaves must be left. In cold climates, chives die back in winter. Chives should be lifted and divided every two to three years in either spring or autumn, or immediately after flowering. Use in fresh salads and to flavour potatoes or any of the marrow family. Chives are good in most savoury dishes and excellent with eggs and cream.

CORIANDER
Sometimes called Chinese parsley or cilantro, coriander is an attractive annual that grows to 60 cm/2 ft. The lacy foliage has a distinctive, strong aroma. Coriander can be grown either in a sunny spot in the garden or indoors in pots on a sunny windowsill. Plant the whole coriander seeds in spring and keep well watered. Harvest seeds in autumn and dry in a light, airy position. When the small oval, coriander seeds have hardened and ripened to a pale fawn colour, they are one of the most deliciously fragrant of all spices used in cooking. Coriander is used in almost every Thai dish. The leaves are tasty in salads and as a garnish for pea soup, while the seeds complement mushrooms, cauliflower, beetroot and celery, and are commonly used in curries, sausage-making and as a flavouring in cakes.

CURRY PLANT
The curry plant is a shrubby perennial plant that grows into a low spreading bush with green spiky leaves. Although it is not used in authentic curries, the leaves do have a strong curry-like flavour.

CURRY LEAVES
These should not be confused with the leaves of the curry plant. Curry leaves are small, shiny and evergreen, and look slightly like small bay leaves. The tree is easily grown and is decorative, with an exotic spicy fragrance. Curry leaves are usually chopped and fried in oil at the start of making curry. They quickly turn brown and become crisp when the other ingredients are added. The leaves may also be used in the making of curry powder and curry paste.

DILL
A fast-growing, upright annual that grows to 90 cm/3 ft, dill resembles fennel in that both have hollow stems, feathery leaves and clusters of yellow flowers. The flavour of dill is clean and delicate. Sow the seeds in a sunny, well-drained soil in spring and autumn. Dill grows best in a light, medium-rich soil with plenty of moisture. Both dill seeds and leaves can be eaten. Dill seed flavours, and helps the digestion of, steamed cabbage, coleslaw, sauerkraut, cucumbers, various chutneys and pickles, pastries, breads, sauces and cooked root vegetables.

FENNEL
This fast-growing, tall annual reaches to 1.5 m/5 ft and has bright green, feathery leaves with clusters of yellow flowers followed by aniseed-flavoured seeds. Grow fennel in a well-drained, sunny position and provide it with plenty of water. Both leaves and seeds are traditionally used with fish. When baking a whole fish, use branches of the foliage as a fragrant bed for the fish to rest on during cooking. Fennel seeds are used in soups and sauces, with lentils, rice and potatoes as well as in breads and cakes. The leaves are also used in salads, relishes and as a garnish.

GARLIC
A bulbous perennial plant with strap-like leaves measuring approximately 2.5 cm/

73

1 in across and 30 cm/1 ft long. Garlic has a willowy, round flower stalk that thrusts upwards above the leaves, and a flower that appears as a compact collection of mauve-tinted white petals. Plant separated cloves in early spring in a rich and well-drained soil, preferably in full sun. When the foliage has died down at the end of the summer, the bulbs can be carefully lifted. Dig the bulbs, shake them free of dirt and plait several together. Hang the plaited garlic in a dry, well-ventilated place. The whole garlic plant has a pungent, lingering odour. The oil has antibiotic properties and contains Vitamins A and B, sulphur and iodine.

HORSERADISH

This hardy perennial has long, elliptical, dark green leaves and grows to a height of about 60 cm/2 ft with erect stems and small, scented, four-petalled white flowers. It is often grown for its thick, fleshy, aromatic roots which are hot, pungent and full of flavour. Plant horseradish in an open sunny position, in a deeply dug, fertile soil. Horseradish sauce uses grated roots mixed with cream or some similar viscous liquid. It must be used raw as the cooked roots lose their flavour. Roots can be grated, then dried and stored in airtight containers for later use. The leaves can be chopped and used as a salad ingredient.

LEMON BALM

A perennial that grows to 90 cm/3 ft, lemon balm has dark green, heart-shaped leaves that have a strong lemon scent and flavour. Grow in a rich, well-drained soil in full sun. Pinch back in early summer to encourage new growth and use fresh leaves sprinkled over vegetable and fruit salads. The leaves are also delicious in fish and poultry dishes, sauces, marinades and stuffings. Lemon balm is sometimes planted in orchards to attract bees to pollinate the fruit blossom.

LEMON GRASS

This grass-like perennial grows to 3 m/9^3/4 ft high and has pointed aromatic leaves with a delicious lemon scent. It will form into a large clump when planted in a sunny, warm position with plenty of water and good drainage. The fleshy white lower part of the leaves is used in many Southeast Asian dishes. It adds a tangy taste to salads and is a must for curries. If fresh lemon grass is called for in a recipe it can be replaced with dried lemon grass or finely grated lemon rind.

MARJORAM

This fragrant perennial plant grows to 75 cm/2^1/2 ft high and has small oval leaves with clusters of white or mauve flowers. Grow in full sun in a well-drained soil and keep trimmed to encourage fresh compact growth. The fresh leaves are used in tomato dishes, with any of the cabbage family and green beans. Marjoram is an excellent addition to spicy meat dishes and can be included in meat sauces for pasta, meat loaves and rice stuffings for vegetables.

MINT

There are many varieties of mint, but spearmint (*Mentha spicata*) and applemint (*Mentha suaveolens*) are the two most commonly used in cooking. Mint is a fast-growing perennial which prefers a rich, moist soil and light shade. Freshly chopped, the leaves are used with peas, new potatoes, zucchini (courgettes) and in mixed green salads. Also good in fruit salads, cooling drinks, jellies, vinegar and lamb sauce.

OREGANO

A small spreading perennial that grows to around 45 cm/1^1/2 ft, oregano has small pungent leaves and tiny white or mauve flowers. Grow in a well-drained soil in a

sunny position. The common confusion between marjoram and oregano can be resolved by realising that the cultivated marjoram comes from the wild oregano, and that the first has a sweet flavour and the second a strong, peppery one. Fresh oregano leaves are used to season salads and many tomato dishes, especially tomato sauces used with pasta. It is also used with eggplant (aubergine), beans, zucchini (courgettes) and cheese.

PARSLEY

This biennial plant grows to 60 cm/2 ft high and has flat or curly leaves. Parsley is grown from seeds which should be sown direct in spring and summer. Parsley likes a rich, well-drained soil in partial or full sun, and responds to frequent feeding. It is one of the most popular herbs of all and can be added to soups, stews, casseroles, sauces and stuffings. Always include the chopped stems as they are full of flavour and nutriment.

ROSEMARY

A Mediterranean evergreen shrub that grows to around 1.5 m/5 ft high. Rosemary has thin, dark-green leaves which are silver on the underside and highly aromatic; the pale blue flowers grow along the stems as well as at the tips. Choose a sheltered sunny spot for planting, preferably against a wall, or in a corner, as rosemary needs all the protection it can get. The leaves are good with meat dishes, particularly lamb. The flavour is strong, so use sparingly.

SAGE

A small perennial shrub with soft, grey-green leaves and blue flowers during summer. Grow in a sunny, well-drained position and trim regularly. Give it plenty of water during summer. The leaves have a strong, clean flavour which combats the greasiness of fatty foods. Chopped fresh sage leaves are delicious in salads, potato dishes and with cheese, but use sparingly. Also use with pork, veal and poultry as well as in seasonings.

SORREL

A perennial that grows to 90 cm/3 ft tall, sorrel has large, bright green, arrow-shaped leaves that have a sharp lemony, bitter taste. It prefers a well-drained, rich soil in sun or semi-shade. The young fresh leaves are excellent in a mixed green salad and a few leaves are delicious when cooked with spinach. Sorrel is used to make classic French sorrel soup and in sauces and vegetable purées.

TARRAGON

French tarragon is a bushy perennial that grows to around 1 m/3 ft high. Its dark slender leaves have a slight anise flavour. It likes a moderately rich, well-drained soil and a sunny position. French tarragon can only be propagated by division. Use tarragon with fish, shellfish, poultry, game, veal, liver, kidneys and in egg dishes. Tarragon vinegar is an essential ingredient in béarnaise sauce.

THYME

This strongly aromatic shrubby perennial grows to around 45 cm/ 1^1/$_2$ ft high. It has tiny, oval leaves and bears pretty pastel-coloured flowers. There are many varieties including lemon thyme, caraway thyme and a pretty variegated type. All thymes like a sunny position with a light, well-drained soil and should be kept trimmed to keep them compact. Thyme is one of the most successful herbs for drying. Use the fresh leaves sparingly with most vegetables including beetroot, tomatoes and zucchini (courgettes). Thyme is also delicious in casseroles, meat dishes, pâtés and stuffings.

AT-A-GLANCE HERB GUIDE

HERB	SOUPS	MAIN DISHES
Basil	Tomato and fish soups	Fish dishes, meat loaf, casseroles
Bay	All soups and stocks	Meat, fish and poultry dishes
Chervil	Fish and vegetable soups	Chicken, egg, cheese dishes, casseroles
Chives	Chilled soups, vichyssoise	Egg dishes, meat and chicken dishes
Coriander – fresh	Chilled soups	Oriental and Middle Eastern cooking, seafood, poultry, meat dishes
Dill – fresh	Fish and vegetable soups	Fish, lamb and pork dishes
Marjoram	Vegetable and meat soups	Casseroles, meat, marinades, meat loaf
Mint	Summer soups	Lamb dishes, trout
Oregano	Minestrone and tomato soups	Italian dishes, pasta and egg dishes, quiches, pizza
Parsley	All soups	All fish, poultry, meat and egg dishes, pasta
Rosemary	Meat stocks, chicken and tomato soups	Lamb and chicken dishes
Sage	Minestrone, chicken, tomato, celery and lentil soups	Meat loaf, pork, cheese and egg dishes
Tarragon	Fish and tomato soups	Fish, chicken and some egg dishes
Thyme	Vegetable and meat soups and stock	Meat, chicken and pasta dishes

VEGETABLE DISHES	DESSERTS AND BAKED PRODUCTS	OTHER USES
Tomato and green salads, baked vegetables dishes		Dips, savouries, herb sandwiches, pasta sauces
Vegetable casseroles	Place a leaf on a baked rice pudding or a baked custard	Flavour pâtés and terrines
Salads, root vegetable dishes	Savoury breads and biscuits	Herb butters, meat sauces
Salads, potato dishes		Dips, herb butters, garnish
Green salads, oriental dishes		Dips, pickles
Especially good with cucumber and cauliflower		Fish sauces, cheese dips
Tomato dishes, potato and vegetable casseroles	Herb scones	Sauces, herb butters, stuffings
New potatoes, peas, carrots, salads	Fruit salads, ice cream	Summer drinks, mint sauce, stuffings
Onions, potatoes, red and green peppers	Herb bread	Pâtés, stuffings
All vegetables and salads	Herb and savoury bread	Dressing, stuffing, garnish for most savoury dishes
Eggplant (aubergines), tomatoes, cabbage	Herb and savoury breads and scones	Dressing, stuffings, dumplings, pâtés
Salads, vegetarian casseroles	Savoury breads and scones	Herbal teas
Mushrooms, carrots, salads		Sauces, stuffings and dressings
Most vegetable dishes		Sauces, stuffings, herbal teas

USEFUL INFORMATION

Can sizes vary between countries and manufacturers. You may find the quantities in this book are slightly different from what is available. Purchase and use the can size nearest to the suggested size in the recipe.

In this book, ingredients such as fish and meat are given in grams so you know how much to buy. It is handy to have:
- A small inexpensive set of kitchen scales.

Other ingredients in our recipes are given in tablespoons and cups, so you will need:
- A nest of measuring cups (1 cup, $1/2$ cup, $1/3$ cup and $1/4$ cup).
- A set of measuring spoons (1 tablespoon, 1 teaspoon, $1/2$ teaspoon and $1/4$ teaspoon).
- A transparent graduated measuring jug (1 litre or 250 mL) for measuring liquids.
- Cup and spoon measures are level.

QUICK CONVERTER

Metric	Imperial
5 mm	$1/4$ in
1 cm	$1/2$ in
2 cm	$3/4$ in
2.5 cm	1 in
5 cm	2 in
10 cm	4 in
15 cm	6 in
20 cm	8 in
23 cm	9 in
25 cm	10 in
30 cm	12 in

MEASURING LIQUIDS

Metric	Imperial	Cup
30 mL	1 fl oz	
60 mL	2 fl oz	$1/4$ cup
90 mL	3 fl oz	
125 mL	4 fl oz	$1/2$ cup
155 mL	5 fl oz	
170 mL	$5^1/2$ fl oz	$2/3$ cup
185 mL	6 fl oz	
220 mL	7 fl oz	
250 mL	8 fl oz	1 cup
500 mL	16 fl oz	2 cups
600 mL	20 fl oz (1 pt)	
750 mL	$1^1/4$ pt	
1 litre	$1^3/4$ pt	4 cups
1.2 litres	2 pt	

METRIC CUPS & SPOONS

Metric	Cups	Imperial
60 mL	$1/4$ cup	2 fl oz
80 mL	$1/3$ cup	$2^1/2$ fl oz
125 mL	$1/2$ cup	4 fl oz
250 mL	1 cup	8 fl oz
	Spoons	
1.25 mL	$1/4$ teaspoon	
2.5 mL	$1/2$ teaspoon	
5 mL	1 teaspoon	
20 mL	1 tablespoon	

MEASURING DRY INGREDIENTS

Metric	Imperial
15 g	$1/2$ oz
30 g	1 oz
60 g	2 oz
90 g	3 oz
125 g	4 oz
155 g	5 oz
185 g	6 oz
220 g	7 oz
250 g	8 oz
280 g	9 oz
315 g	10 oz
375 g	12 oz
410 g	13 oz
440 g	14 oz
470 g	15 oz
500 g	16 oz (1 lb)
750 g	1 lb 8 oz
1 kg	2 lb
1.5 kg	3 lb

OVEN TEMPERATURES

°C	°F	Gas Mark
120	250	$1/2$
140	275	1
150	300	2
160	325	3
180	350	4
190	375	5
200	400	6
220	425	7
240	475	8
250	500	9

INDEX

UK COOKERY EDITOR
Katie Swallow

EDITORIAL
Food Editor: Rachel Blackmore
Editorial Assistant: Ella Martin
Editorial Co-ordinator: Margaret Kelly
Recipe Development: Sheryle Eastwood, Lucy Kelly, Voula
Maritzouridis, Anneka Mitchell, Penelope Peel, Belinda Warn,
Loukie Werle
Credits: Recipes page 12 by Jackie Passmore; pages 52, 54, 61, 70, 71
by Annette Grimsdale; pages 53, 54, 55 by Mary Nowark; page 68
Gordon Grimsdale; page 69 June Budgen © Merehurst Limited

COVER
Photography: Ashley Mackevicius
Styling: Wendy Berecry

PHOTOGRAPHY
Per Ericson, Ray Joyce, Ashley Mackevicius, Harm Mol, Yanto
Noerianto, Jon Stewart, Warren Webb, Philip Wymant

STYLING
Wendy Berecry, Belinda Clayton, Rosemary De Santis,
Jacqui Hing, Michelle Gorry

DESIGN AND PRODUCTION
Manager: Sheridan Carter
Layout and Finished Art: Lulu Dougherty
Design: Frank Pithers

Published by J.B. Fairfax Press Pty Limited
Formatted by J.B. Fairfax Press Pty Limited
Output by Adtype, Sydney
Printed by Toppan Printing Co, Singapore

© J.B. Fairfax Press Pty Limited, 1993
This book is copyright. No part may be reproduced or transmitted
without the written permission of the publisher. Enquiries should be
made in writing to the publisher.

174 UK
Includes Index
ISBN 1 86343 047 4 (pbk)
ISBN 1 85391 279 4

Distributed by J.B. Fairfax Press Ltd
9 Trinity Centre, Park Farm Estate
Wellingborough, Northants, UK
Ph: (0933) 402330 Fax: (0933) 402234